A Masterpiece of Counterguerrilla Warfare: BG J. Franklin Bell in the Philippines, 1901–1902

OP 25

Robert D. Ramsey III

Combat Studies Institute Press
US Army Combined Arms Center
Fort Leavenworth, Kansas

Library of Congress Cataloging-in-Publication Data

Ramsey, Robert D., 1946-
  A masterpiece of counterguerrilla warfare : BG J. Franklin Bell in the
Philippines, 1901-1902 / by Robert D. Ramsey III.
    p. cm. -- (Long war series occasional paper ; 25) 1. Bell, James Franklin,
1856-1919 2. Counterinsurgency. 3. Counterinsurgency--United States--
History--19th century. 4. Philippines--History--Philippine American War,
1899-1902. I. Bell, James Franklin, 1856-1919 Telegraphic circulars. II. Lieber,
Francis, 1800-1872. Instructions for the government of armies of the United
States in the field. III. Title. IV. Title: J. Franklin Bell in the Philippines, 1901-
1902. V. Series.

  U241.R36 2007
  959.9'031--dc22

                                                    2007042624

CSI Press publications cover a variety of military history topics. The views expressed in this CSI Press publication are those of the author(s) and not necessarily those of the Department of the Army or the Department of Defense. A full list of CSI Press publications, many of them available for downloading, can be found at http://usacac.army.mil/CAC/csi/RandP/CSIpubs.asp.

For sale by the Superintendent of Documents, U.S. Government Printing Office
Internet: bookstore.gpo.gov Phone: toll free (866) 512-1800; DC area (202) 512-1800
Fax: (202) 512-2104 Mail: Stop IDCC, Washington, DC 20402-0001

ISBN 978-0-16-079503-9

Foreword

Combat Studies Institute (CSI) presents Long War Series Occasional Paper (OP) 25, *A Masterpiece of Counterguerrilla Warfare: BG J. Franklin Bell in the Philippines, 1901–1902,* by Robert Ramsey. OP 25 is a companion to OP 24, *Savage Wars of Peace: Case Studies of Pacification in the Philippines, 1900–1902.* In OP 24 Ramsey analyzed case studies from two different Philippine military districts discovering several themes relevant to today's ongoing operations in the Long War. In OP 25 he focuses on the philosophy that guided Bell in the conduct of one of those campaigns.

Over the ages military historians have employed many types of research and writing to understand, and ultimately learn from, the past. These methods range from studies of grand strategy to studies of small unit tactics to, most recently, studies of the history of war and society. OP 25 takes a different approach, one whose origins are old and rather infrequently practiced today. This technique examines the inner thinking of a commander in an attempt to understand how he viewed the operation he was conducting. In reading Bell's words today, it becomes clear he displayed at least two of the key attributes that constitute Clausewitz's concept of military genius—the inner light or vision that points a commander toward victory in the fog of war and the determination to act decisively in the face of danger.

Mr. Ramsey, in his introduction, makes note of British Field Marshal Sir Archibald P. Wavell's endorsement of this kind of history: "The real way to get value out of the study of military history is to take particular situations, and as far as possible get inside the skin of the man who made a decision, realize the conditions in which the decision was made, and then see in what way you could have improved upon it." This quote captures the intent of this study.

The collected messages and circulars issued by Bell to his subordinate commanders, and the text of the US Army's famous General Orders 100 from which he drew that guidance, provide the means to accomplish what Clausewitz and Wavell urged us to do. We believe this Occasional Paper will be a valuable addition to the education of all military professionals. *CSI—The Past Is Prologue!*

Timothy R. Reese
Colonel, Armor
Director, Combat Studies Institute

Contents

Introduction

The contrast between the campaigns of Generals Bell and Smith was striking in almost every important element. Bell's operation, unlike Smith's, was a credit to the American Army in the Philippines and a masterpiece of counter-guerrilla warfare.

John M. Gates (1973)[1]

Both Smith and Bell waged particularly ruthless campaigns of concentration and mass destruction. . . . Of the two campaigns, Bell's was better organized and quickly won acclaim throughout the Army as a model counterinsurgency operation.

Andrew J. Birtle (1998)[2]

Indeed, one of the few things both MacArthur and Taft agreed on was that Bell was the most outstanding general in the archipelago. . . . In a series of field and telegraphic orders and in a . . . speech to his top subordinates Bell outlined the most coherent and well-organized pacification campaign of the war.

Brian M. Linn (2000)[3]

During research for the Long War Series Occasional Paper 24, *Savage Wars of Peace: Case Studies of Pacification in the Philippine, 1900–1902*, a copy of *Telegraphic Circulars and General Orders, Regulating Campaign Against Insurgents and Proclamations and Circular Letters, Relating to Reconstruction after Close of War in the Provinces of Batangas, Laguna, and Mindoro, Philippine Islands* (hereafter *Telegraphic Circulars and General Orders*) issued by Brigadier General J. Franklin Bell was located in the archives of the Combined Arms Research Library at Fort Leavenworth, Kansas. Commenting on the reluctance of the US Army to address its experiences in the Philippine Insurrection,[4] a historian from the Center of Military History noted:

> One of the most serious casualties in this process was the *Telegraphic Circulars*, a compilation of the orders that General Bell had issued during the final Batangas campaign. The pamphlet was a gem reminiscent of Crook's Resume of Operations Against Apache Indians, in that it contained not only Bell's orders, but also a discussion of

his counterinsurgency philosophy. Although the pamphlet was inserted into the record by a congressional committee investigating the war, the Army itself did not distribute it beyond the archipelago, allegedly because of the sensitivity of the subject matter.[5]

To address this shortcoming, the Combat Studies Institute Press decided to reprint Bell's *Telegraphic Circulars and General Orders* along with General Orders 100, "Instructions for the Government of Armies of the United States in the Field." Although written over a hundred years ago, these documents provide insights for today's military professionals into how an experienced brigade commander successfully tackled a difficult counterguerrilla situation.

Brigadier General James Franklin Bell

J. Franklin Bell, "probably the finest Army commander in the Philippine War,"[6] served continuously in the Philippines from 1898 to 1902. Born in Kentucky in 1856, Bell became a cavalry second lieutenant on graduation from the US Military Academy in 1878. Posted to the 7th Cavalry after the Little Big Horn disaster, Bell served in various regimental assignments for almost 20 years. From 1886 to 1889, he was the Professor of Military Science and Tactics at Southern Illinois University. While there, he studied law and was admitted to the bar. Assigned to the 7th Cavalry at the end of 1890, Bell was promoted to first lieutenant. He served as aide to the commander of the Department of California from 1894 to 1897 before returning to regimental duty at Fort Apache, Arizona, in 1897. At the outbreak of the Spanish-American War, Bell became a major of volunteers and the engineer officer for the Philippine-bound VIII Corps forming in San Francisco.[7]

Bell, one of the first American soldiers to arrive in the Philippines, served as the VIII Corps chief of military information or intelligence officer. In 1898, he earned a reputation for daring and competence during personal reconnaissances of the Spanish defenses of Manila. In addition, Bell worked with many leaders of the Philippine resistance at Manila. When the Philippine Insurrection broke out in early 1899, Bell, assigned as the engineer of the 2d Division, aggressively led numerous reconnaissance operations during the spring campaign north of Manila. Time after time Bell found weaknesses in the *insurrecto* defensive positions and exploited them to the benefit of the American forces. In March, still serving as a major of volunteers, Bell was promoted to Regular Army captain in the 7th Cavalry after over 20 years of service. In the summer of 1899, Bell became a colonel of volunteers. He raised, trained, and commanded the 36th US Volunteer (USV) Infantry Regiment, one of two infantry regiments created in the Philippines from discharged veterans of the departing state volunteer regiments. A subordinate who served in the 36th USV Infantry and who retired as a major general after World War I wrote, "In all my service since, I have never known an officer who was held in such high regard by the officers and men of his command as was Colonel Bell."[8] He credited the 36th USV Infantry's accomplishments during the fall 1899 campaign to Bell's

> . . . uncanny ability . . . to value correctly the powers and limitations of the enemy, and to the professional knowledge and courage to take advantage of his weaknesses. The Colonel organized, equipped, and trained the 36th Infantry for the character of service it was to be called to perform. But behind it all was the Colonel's exceptionally able leadership of men in war. The officers and men loved him personally. They had almost divine confidence in his military judgment and decisions. They whole-heartedly did whatever he suggested without a doubt of its correctness. Accompanying this he had the ability to convey to the officers and men his views and policies, instruction, and directions in a quickly understandable manner.[9]

Bell earned the Medal of Honor leading an attack near the town of Proac in September 1899. With the dispersal of the *insurrecto* army in November and the end of combat operations, the 36th USV Infantry occupied Pangasinan province.

In December Bell was promoted to brigadier general of volunteers and assigned command of the 4th Brigade of the 2d Division, which was reorganized in early 1900 as a district under the Department of Northern Luzon. As district commander Bell noted that in addition to the routine tasks of taking care of soldiers, gathering intelligence on activities throughout the district, and establishing security by pursuing *insurrectos* or bandits, his duties included:

> . . . apprehension, collection of evidence, trial, disposition, and imprisonment of criminals; the re-establishment of civil government, of schools, mail, and telegraphic communications; the re-construction of roads and bridges; the collection of revenue taxes and insular statistics; supervising the affairs of provincial

and municipal governments; the investigation of claims of all descriptions; and the discharge of all other duties heretofore performed by civil officials.[10]

Bell, and many American commanders, found that pacification and occupation duties in the midst of an alien and unfriendly population proved "far more onerous . . . than they were when the insurrection was in its greatest activity."[11]

By mid-1900, Bell found himself assigned as the Provost Marshal General in Manila, responsible for security within the city. In that position, just as during the siege and battle for Manila in 1898, Bell worked closely with the Filipinos. In December 1900, Major General Arthur MacArthur, the Philippine Division commander, instituted martial law throughout the Philippines under provisions of General Orders 100[12] and began a harsher, less benevolent pacification campaign.[13] At that time, Bell addressed his officers in Manila that he had often heard the opinion "that no good had been accomplished"[14] by the previous benevolent pacification policy but that

> I cannot concur in that opinion, for I feel convinced that this policy has had a good effect. Had we been building for a day only or solely in order to put an end to hostilities, a different policy might have been indicated, but . . . we have got to continue to live among these people. We have got to govern them. Government by force alone cannot be satisfactory to Americans. It is desirable that a Government be established in time which is based upon the will of the governed. This can be accomplished satisfactorily only by obtaining and retaining the good will of the people. . . . Our policy heretofore was calculated to prevent the birth of undying resentment and hatred. This policy has earned for us the respect and approval of a large majority of the more intelligent and influential portion of the community. We cannot lose their support by now adopting measures as may be necessary to suppress the irreconcilable and disorderly.[15]

Bell described the new policy to his officers as not one of "harsh and indiscriminate persecution," but one of "considerate firmness" directed against those Filipinos who opposed American pacification.[16]

In February 1901, Bell became the youngest brigadier general in the US Army when promoted directly from Regular Army captain to Regular Army brigadier general. At the same time, he was assigned to command ongoing operations in the First District, Department of Northern Luzon, located in the Ilocano region of northwest Luzon. Bell continued his predecessor's pressure against the *insurrecto* infrastructure in the towns and against the guerrilla bands in the countryside. Resistance ended there on 1 May.[17] Reflecting the attitude of the time, Bell reported that Filipinos

> . . . are the most skillful dissimulators on earth, and many of our officers, fresh from the States, had the wool so completely pulled over their eyes as to be incompetent to cope with these able deceivers. They have a great many good qualities but a wonderful lot of customs and habits which must be trained out of them before we should ever be able to make a creditable people of them.[18]

Despite this general view of Filipinos, Bell's primary role in the Ilocos campaign has been described as being "willing and able to escalate the war to a level that the revolutionary leaders found intolerable and, once they surrendered . . . to reconcile them to American rule."[19] Bell remained in command of First District until November 1901.

Bell's Counterguerrilla Campaign in Southwestern Luzon, 1901–1902

On 28 September 1901 at Balangiga on the island of Samar, *insurrectos* commanded by Vincene Lukban attacked and destroyed the 74-man American military garrison resulting in 44 killed, 22 wounded, 4 missing, and 4 uninjured. The Governor of the Philippines, William H. Taft, and the Philippine Division commander, Major General Adna R. Chaffee, responded to the "Balangiga massacre" with military operations designed to end *insurrecto* resistance on Samar and Luzon once and for all. To conduct these operations, Chaffee chose two of his most experienced, capable, and proven commanders: Brigadier General Jacob H. Smith to destroy Lukban's *insurrectos* on Samar and Bell to end the resistance of Miguel Malvar and his subordinate Pedro Caballes in the Tagalog region of southwestern Luzon to include the provinces of Batangas, Laguna, and portions of Tayabas (see map). Both Smith and Bell employed similar methods, but in different manners. Both were successful in ending *insurrecto* resistance in their areas of operations. "Hell-Roaring Jake" Smith's campaign on Samar generated criticism that led to a Congressional inquiry and to courts-martial. In contrast, Bell's campaign—described by historians as "a masterpiece of counter-guerrilla warfare," "a model counterinsurgency operation," and "the most coherent and well-organized pacification" conducted in the Philippines—was praised by both civilian and military leaders.

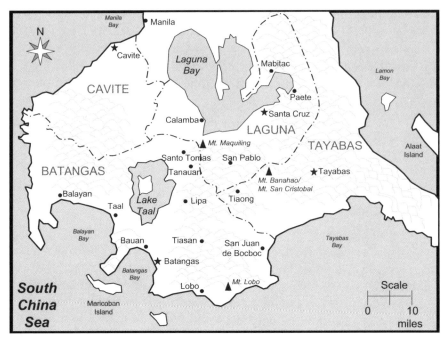

Map of Tagalog region.

Bell's new assignment was fraught with difficulties. A member of the Philippine Commission noted that Bell indicated he

> . . . was under specific orders, which while they seem necessary, do not furnish him an especially agreeable task. . . . [He] is sent to Batangas to make peace, and he proposes to do so even if the peace which he establishes must be the peace of desolation. He seemed to be in a somewhat reflective and subdued frame of mind in the presence of an undertaking which might bring destruction to a once rich province and great suffering to a large body of people. While the task is not of his choosing, it is clear that although he may expect to be vilified and have to bear the responsibility of action in many cases which he cannot control, still he seemed to have a deep determination to carry out his orders and to end rebellion in Batangas.[20]

Despite his misgivings, Bell was determined to accomplish his assigned mission in the 3d Separate Brigade area of operations as quickly and as completely as possible.

With 3-years' experience in the Philippines, Bell understood that what worked in one region did not always work in another. Initially, he gathered information to understand the specific problem in his brigade area. Bell spent his first week interviewing "every prominent Filipino within my reach who had the reputation of really desiring peace" and concluded "that the only way that I could possibly succeed in putting an end to insurrection within the territorial limits of the brigade would be by cutting off the income and food of the insurgents, and by crowding them so persistently with operations as to wear them out."[21] At the port of Batangas on 1 December, Bell met with his officers to explain what he had learned from his experience in the Philippines, what his initial assessment of the problem in the brigade area of operations was, and what he intended to do under martial law in accordance with General Orders 100.[22]

Bell's basic concept of operations was to separate the population from the guerrilla units through a series of measures designed to concentrate the population in protected zones near the major towns and to attack the *insurrecto* infrastructure in the towns during December. This was to be followed on 1 January 1902 by increased combat operations to maintain pressure on the guerrilla bands. On 6 December, Bell issued the first of 38 telegraphic circulars to his post commanders that set the conditions for success against both the *insurrecto* infrastructure in the towns and guerrillas in the field. During December, Bell issued 24 of his telegraphic circulars before increased combat activity commenced. The range of activities and the specific instructions the telegraphic circulars provided to his post commanders showed Bell's grasp of how he intended to attack both the *insurrecto* infrastructure and the guerrilla bands. The circulars demonstrated his method of ensuring both his subordinates and the local populace understood these instructions, their legal basis in General Orders 100, and his expectations of compliance. Unlike Smith's operations on Samar, Bell's campaign "was highly organized . . . [he] maintained control of the overall direction of operations at all times. Determined that the Filipinos should not misunderstand the American policy, he impressed upon his officers the importance of warning the people before instituting any repressive measures."[23]

On 26 December 1901, Bell provided his immediate superior, Major General Loyd Wheaton, an update on the status of his preparations. In his lengthy telegram, Bell also provided his concept for the counterguerrilla operations that were to commence on 1 January 1902.

General WHEATON, *Manila*:

Your message requiring my opinion as to the benefit of peace negotiations by Manila and other conspirators in suppression of insurrection in Batangas is received. Respectfully report that I have become convinced that within two months at the outside there will be no more insurrection in this brigade, and nothing for conspirators to negotiate about. We may not have secured all the guns or caught all the insurgents by that time, and the present insurrection will end and the men and the guns will be secured in time. My only fear is that they will bury their guns and scatter, sneaking away individually into other provinces to await a more favorable temperature at home, or they may march with their guns northward into Morong, Bulacan, or Nueva Ecija [provinces], or southeastward into General Grant's brigade. I am practically sure they can not remain here in Batangas, Laguna, and a part of Tayabas. The people are now assembled in the towns, with all the visible food supply, except that cached by insurgents in mountains. For the next six days all station commanders will be employed hunting insurgents and their hidden food supplies within their respective jurisdictions. Population of each town will be turned out, and all transportation that can be found impressed to bring into Government storehouses all food that is found, if it be possible to transport it. If not, it will be destroyed.

I am now assembling in the neighborhood of 2,500 men, who will be used in columns of about 50 men each. I expect to accompany this command. Of course no such strength is necessary to cope with all the insurgents in the Philippine Islands, but the country is indescribably rough and badly cut up, the ravines and mountains. I take so large a command for the purpose of thoroughly searching each ravine, valley, and mountain peak for insurgents and for food, expecting to destroy everything I find outside of towns, all able-bodied men will be killed or captured. Old men, women, and children will be sent to towns. This movement begins January 1, by which time I hope to have nearly all the food supply in the towns. If insurgents hide their guns and come into the towns it will be to my advantage, for I shall put such a pressure on town officials and police that they will be compelled to identify insurgents. If I catch these I shall get their guns in time. I expect to first clean out the wide Loboo peninsula south of Batangas, Tiasan, and San Juan de Boc Boc road. I shall then move command to the vicinity of Lake Taal and sweep the country westward to the ocean and south of Cavite; returning through Lipa, I shall scour and clean up the Lipa Mountains; swinging northward, the country in the vicinity of San Pablo, Alaminos, Tanauan, and Santo Tomas will be scoured, ending at Mount Maquiling, which will then be thoroughly searched and devastated. This is said to be the home of Malvar and his parents.

Swinging back to the right, the same treatment will be given all the country of which Mount Cristobal and Mount Banahao are the main peaks. These two mountains, Mount Maquiling, and the mountains northeast of Loboo are the main haunts of the insurgents. After the 1st of January no one will be permitted to move about without pass. I shall keep the country full of scouting detachments and give insurgents no peace. I feel morally certain that they can not stand the strain and the lack of food that will ensue for two months. The ten companies of the Ninth Cavalry would be most valuable in these operations. If this does not bring about a surrender we will get the guns and insurgents also little by little. We have several towns on our side begging for mercy and organizing in opposition to insurgents. They have formed volunteer companies to control their towns and have notified insurgents that they must surrender or the people themselves intend to join the Americans in their operations.

The insurgent army in this province was made of town contingents, each town being supplied with so many guns and being required to maintain so many soldiers. All the guns, except about a dozen formerly pertaining to the town of Bauan, have already been captured by Captain Hartman, mainly through the efforts of the townspeople themselves. This was the first town on which Captain Boughton laid his heavy hand as brigade provost-marshal and provost court. We expect to have every town in these provinces in the same attitude shortly. As for peace commissioners, if Sixto Lopez or any other man of equal influence could be trusted to work honestly and sincerely, there is no doubt but what he could bring about peace, for, with few exceptions, it can be now truthfully said that everybody wants peace, even the insurgents. Malvar and a few irreconcilables like himself may not be ready to cry quits, but insurgent soldiers are coming in every day claiming to have been serving involuntarily and to have escaped from their leaders. They come in notwithstanding they know they will go into the carcel. Despite these conditions, however, it is doubtful if any peace commission, from Aguinaldo down, could secure a thorough surrender of all the guns. The breaking away at the last minute of disaffected parties would occur as it did in the Cailles surrender, or all the best guns would be buried or concealed. Such results following a peace brought about by peace commissioners prior to the suffering by these people of the real hardships of war would almost certainly be followed by another insurrection within the next five years.

These people need a thrashing to teach them some good common sense, and they should have it for the good of all concerned. Sixto Lopez is now interested in peace because I have in jail all the male members of his family found in my jurisdiction, and have seized his houses and palay and his steamer, the *Purisima Concepcion*, for use of the Government. As for the peace commissioners sent by the Manila Peace League, they have accomplished nothing that I know of. Paterno got 30 passes, good for anybody to whom he chose to give or send them, as they were only numbered, in order that they might be good in anyone's hands in which he or his agents might place them. I fear that a number of insurgent officers who have committed barbarous crimes may have availed themselves of these passes to escape from the country. This may possibly be a necessary preliminary to success on the part of the peace commissioners. Paterno stated in his letter of application that he wanted to furnish each messenger with three passes. Notwithstanding all these passes expire December 31, the only peace commissioner who reported himself to me prior to December 19 was Señor Velarde, who about the middle of the month reported himself at Calamba, and within a few days thereafter telegraphed me that he had returned to Manila on business with the Peace League. On the above date, December 19, six peace commissioners arrived here on the *Ysla de Negros*, a chartered transport, with seven passes. It looked to me as though a number of men had managed to get themselves back into closed ports on the passes.

The names of the six were taken from the manifest, and they were permitted to go about their business, whereupon they immediately disappeared. It was then discovered that one of the six men named on the manifest, Mariano Mendoza, had not come, but that one, Luciano Lucas, whom I remember as an irreconcilable prisoner of war when I was provost-marshal-general, had come in his place. He had been insurgent colonel under Pio del Pilar, and while a prisoner at Postigo was several times reported to me as an insurgent agitator among the prisoners. The citizen, Williams, whom the division commander sent here, informed me that this Luciano Lucas, after having been released at Manila and taking the oath of allegiance, had come here to Batangas and had smuggled his way to Mindoro on a mission to the insurgents while Williams was there. A native who served me at Manila, an exceptionally intelligent and strong-minded man, was sent down to assist me by Buen Camino. I asked him to ascertain and let me know what these six peace commissioners were doing. He could locate but two of them, who had gone to Bauab, and stated that they were very deliberate in their movements; notwithstanding it was then the 23d of December and their passes expired on January 1, they had as yet done nothing, but they were proposing to find the insurgents and offer to make peace with them for the Government on the basis of immunity for all past crimes.

It is needless for me to add that I have little faith in the success of peace commissioners who are sent out by such unscrupulous tricksters as Paterno, Poblete, et al.

J.F. Bell,
Brigadier-General, Commanding.[24]

11

By the time military operations began in earnest at the beginning of January 1902, many guerrilla bands had been scattered. Bell reported that after 10 January, no significant military clash with *insurrecto* guerrillas occurred in the brigade area of operations.[25] Isolated from their support structure in the towns, the guerrillas were run to ground and the countryside stripped of supplies to sustain them. At the same time, the *insurrecto* infrastructure in the towns was systematically attacked.

Insurrectos began surrendering almost immediately. As military operations cleared Batangas and Laguna provinces, guerrillas fled into the mountains of northern and western Tayabas province. Bell, personally supervising operations in the field, pursued the guerrillas wherever they went. On 11 February he reported his findings of *insurrecto* activity in parts of the civilian administered and supposedly pacified province of Tayabas.

BATANGAS, *February 11, 1902—12.25 p.m.*

ADJUTANT-GENERAL DEPARTMENT NORTH PHILIPPINES, *Manila*:

Finished my inspection of the towns in province of Tayabas yesterday morning, and leaving there arrived here last night in order to start Eleventh Cavalry into the field promptly. Political conditions in Tayabas exceedingly unsatisfactory. Have given orders to commanding officer of towns requiring the adoption and enforcement in full of measures which have been efficacious in Batangas, and the adoption of which was heretofore left to their discretion in Tayabas. There is no possible question but what Laguna insurgents have been encouraged to continue the struggle by their ability to get food supplies from towns in Tayabas and from Manila, through the open ports of Tayabas. Their ability to do this has led many insurgents to flee from Batangas and Laguna to Tayabas, which province they use as a base of operations in Laguna and Batangas.

An insurgent government has also been organized at Binangonan, province of Infanta, and agents sent to communicate with Malvar and Caballes. Stringent measures are necessary in Tayabas and will be fully taken within the limits of my authority. I expect to return to Tayabas with a large field command just as soon as the last stretch of country in Batangas has been fully searched and cleaned up, namely, the stretch of territory between Calamba-Batangas road and eastern shore of Lake Taal. I came back here on horseback, and while riding through San Juan de Boc Boc met Luis Luna, Malvar's adjutant-general, coming in to see the commanding officer about surrendering. Had conference with him. Was willing to surrender unconditionally, but had no arms. Was informed that he would have to remain a prisoner of war until he surrendered his entire following. Stated that being only chief of staff of Malvar, from who he separated January 22, he had no men under his control, but offered to use his influence to do whatever he could to bring about the pacification and render any service I might stipulate in turn for his liberty. He offered to hunt for Malvar and try to influence him to surrender. Authorized commanding officer, San Juan de Boc Boc, to let him go with another native here, hunting for Malvar.

I feel much encouraged to believe that if the ports of Tayabas could be suddenly closed without warning that this measure, in conjunction with those I have already adopted, might convince Caballes and Malvar of the futility of further continuance of the struggle, and something beneficial might result. It is also possible that the insurrection can be brought to an end without closing the ports of Tayabas, but it is worse in that portion which lies in the Fourth Brigade than it is in this. Halfway measures only tend to prolong the war, and vigorous measures were never more desirable, even though the war might be ended in time without them. Respectfully recommend that all ports in province of Tayabas be closed until further orders and that I be authorized, in case I find it necessary, to push my operations into the southern and eastern portion of the province of Tayabas, now included in Fourth Brigade. After I whip them out of the western end they can subsist themselves in the eastern end unless the same measures are adopted to prevent it which now exist in my brigade. I expect to leave here again in a few days.

J.F. Bell, Brigadier-General.[26]

Counterguerrilla operations did not occupy all of Bell's attention. He continued to issue telegraphic circulars to post commanders regarding treatment of the population and prescribed actions to ensure the destruction of the *insurrecto* infrastructure in the towns. On 16 April Malvar, one of the last *insurrecto* holdouts, surrendered. By mid-May Bell declared the resistance ended, reopened the ports to commerce, and on 23 June returned control of Batangas and Laguna provinces to civil government.[27]

Military and civilian leaders in the Philippines considered Bell's campaign "pacification in its most perfected form"[28] and recognized it as "the most thorough and complete district pacification" during the Philippine Insurrection:

> Using telegraphic circulars to enunciate his policies, Bell implemented a complete counterinsurgency campaign designed to separate the guerrillas from the population. He established population reconcentration zones, sent large expeditions into guerrilla strongholds, used provost marshals to break up town infrastructures, destroyed food supplies, and forced the native elite to commit themselves to the Army. These counterinsurgency policies had their desired effect, and guerrilla resistance collapsed within a few months.[29]

At the time, Army officers in the Philippines requested copies of Bell's telegraphic circulars. In response to this demand, in December 1902 they were published, along with other materials, as *Telegraphic Circulars and General Orders*.[30] In 1903, the Philippine Commission passed a reconcentration act capturing Bell's procedures in Philippine law for use in areas with chronic lawlessness.[31]

However, Congressional hearings generated by Smith's operations on Samar tainted Bell's campaign. Bell felt compelled to write a Senator that he believed "what I was doing was the most humane thing I could do under the circumstances, and that my policy was inspired by sympathy and kindness and not by resentment or a desire to punish."[32] In a cover letter to a copy of the *Telegraphic Circulars* that he sent to Secretary of War Elihu Root, Bell stated, "Everything I did during the campaign in Batangas, and nearly always the motive therefore, is indicated in the enclosed small pamphlet. . . . I gave no verbal orders or authority for anything not authorized in this pamphlet. I should be gratified if you would find time to personally read it."[33] Root responded: "I hope you will give yourself no uneasiness regarding the appreciation and approval which our course in the Batangas campaign receives from the War Department. An examination of the orders issued by you has developed no reason for changing the opinion expressed in a telegram [conveying President Roosevelt's congratulations] immediately after the surrender of Malvar."[34]

Shortly thereafter Bell began a 4-year tour as commandant of the Army Service Schools at Fort Leavenworth, Kansas. On 14 April 1906 Bell became Chief of Staff of the US Army. He was promoted to major general in January 1907. During his 4-year tenure as Chief of Staff, he secured an increase in the size of the Army and the Reserves, commanded the Army of Cuban Pacification, and oversaw the relief efforts after the San Francisco earthquake. He returned to Manila to serve as the Department of the Philippines commander from 1911 to 1914. From 1914 to 1915 Bell commanded an experimental 2d Division (Tactical) that assembled at San Antonio, Texas. He went on to command the Western Department from 1915 to 1917, the Eastern Department in 1917, Camp Upton and the 77th Division from 1917 to 1918, and the Eastern Department until his death on 8 January 1919.[35] In 1958, the new home of the US Army Command and General Staff College (CGSC) at Fort Leavenworth, Kansas, was named the J. Franklin Bell Hall. The CGSC resided there until 2007.

Bell's Campaign Instructions

The following documents provide a unique opportunity to follow advice offered in 1930 by Field Marshal Wavell: "The real way to get value out of the study of military history is to take particular situations, and as far as possible get inside the skin of the man who made a decision, realize the conditions in which the decision was made, and then see in what way you could have improved upon it."[36]

Section I, Bell's Telegraphic Circulars and General Orders

Demand from officers in the 3d Separate Brigade and throughout the Philippines for copies of Bell's telegraphic circulars prompted Captain Milton F. Davis, Bell's adjutant, to compile the materials that were published 1 December 1902 as *Telegraphic Circulars and General Orders* (section I). Davis organized the work into nine parts: a topical index to the telegraphic circulars, an explanation (by Davis) of the genesis of the collection, an introduction that consisted of a transcript of Bell's 1 December 1901 address to the officers of the brigade, the 38 telegraphic circulars issued to post commanders between 6 December 1901 and 16 May 1902, a telegraphic memorandum on vaccinations, selected General Orders, proclamations and circular letters issued between May and July 1902, an appendix with thanks for assistance and congratulations to the 3d Separate Brigade for its success, and memoranda by Bell of his reflections or lessons learned during the campaign.

Each part provides information useful for understanding how Bell saw his problem, how he crafted a solution, and how he sequenced his operations against both the guerrilla bands in the countryside and their support infrastructure in the towns. Three sections are critical to understanding the campaign. First, the transcript of Bell's meeting with his officers provides his analysis of the problem, intent, and use of General Orders 100 as the military or martial law within the brigade area. Second, the telegraphic circulars demonstrate Bell's attention to detail, his repeated referral to articles of General Orders 100 to justify and explain his actions to his commanders and the populace, his sequencing of operations in moving the populace into protected zones in preparation of the battlefield for intensified combat operations, and his methodical adjustments to tighten pressure on the *insurrectos*. Last, Bell's memoranda at the end of the publication provides his reflections on the campaign with explanations of what worked and what could have been done better.

Section II, General Orders 100

Bell, just as other American commanders in the Philippines, relied on the Lieber Code or General Orders 100, "Instructions for the Government of Armies of the United States in the Field" (section II), as the basis for martial law. Written during the American Civil War, this internationally recognized code placed requirements and restrictions on an occupying army and on an occupied populace. Failure by either to meet its requirements provided justification for action with loss of rights and protections. Bell, a member of the bar in Illinois, used the provisions of General Orders 100 not to limit what he could do, but to define what he was required to do. For example, a fundamental tenet underlying General Orders 100 was "the notion that an occupier had a moral obligation to protect the people under its control from undue hardship and to provide them with basic governmental services."[37] This duty to protect became Bell's justification for concentrating the population into what he called protected zones near American-controlled towns. In his telegraphic circulars, Bell frequently referred to specific articles of General Orders 100 to explain the legal basis of his actions; to ensure compliance by his commanders; and to educate the Filipino populace on its duties, responsibilities, and liabilities for non-compliance under martial law. To understand *Telegraphic Circulars and General Orders*, it is necessary to comprehend the appropriate articles of General Orders 100. For this reason, General Orders 100 has been provided in section II, and the articles Bell referred to in the *Telegraphic Circulars and General Orders* are identified in **bold type**.

Summary

Today the American military is conducting counterinsurgency operations in Afghanistan and Iraq, and recently the Army chief of staff described the future of the military as one of persistent conflict. This reprint of *Telegraphic Circulars and General Orders* and General Orders 100 provides a unique opportunity to explore insights for today by examining the thinking and actions of Brigadier General J. Franklin Bell in a campaign described as "a masterpiece of counter-guerrilla warfare."[38] Topics to consider include how Bell sought to understand the problem in his area of operations, what he concluded and how he addressed that problem, how he structured and sequenced his concept of operations to separate the population from the guerrillas, how he ensured his intent was understood by his commanders and the populace, how he used General Orders 100 to define and explain what Americans and Filipinos must and could not do, how he supervised the campaign, and what lessons he learned. While some of the methods used by Bell would be unpopular or not permissible today, the value to be gained from studying Bell's telegraphic circulars comes from focusing not so much on what Bell did, but from focusing on his analysis and instructions.

Notes

1. John M. Gates, *Schoolbooks and Krags: The United States Army in the Philippines, 1898–1902* (Westport, CT: Greenwood Press Inc., 1973), 263.

2. Andrew J. Birtle, *US Army Counterinsurgency and Contingency Operations Doctrine, 1860–1941* (Washington, DC: US Army Center of Military History, 1998), 134.

3. Brian M. Linn, *The Philippine War, 1899–1902* (Lawrence, KS: University of Kansas Press, 2000), 300–301.

4. The term "Philippine Insurrection" meant the Filipino rebellion or resistance against American rule. The term had a broader meaning than the term "insurgency" does today. The Philippine Insurrection had two phases: a conventional phase of American army against Filipino army and a longer guerrilla phase of American army against Filipino guerrillas. During both phases, the Filipino fighters were called *insurrectos*.

5. Birtle, 138–139. Birtle is correct in that most of Bell's telegraphic circulars were included in the Congressional records. However, as its full title suggests, the *Telegraphic Circulars and General Orders* published in the Philippines in December 1902 contains more than the telegraphic circulars issued by Bell. Bell's "counterinsurgency philosophy," addressed in the *Telegraphic Circulars and General Orders* but not in the Congressional record, included an address Bell made to the officers of the 3d Separate Brigade on 1 December 1901 and a memoranda Bell wrote after the campaign reflecting lessons learned.

6. Brian M. Linn, *The U.S. Army and Counterinsurgency in the Philippine War, 1899–1902* (Chapel Hill, NC: The University of North Carolina Press, 1989), 59.

7. For an overview of Bell's military career, see http://www.army.mil/cmh-pg/books/cg%26csa/Bell-JF.htm (accessed 4 October 2007).

8. Ewing E. Booth, *My Observations and Experiences in the United States Army* (Los Angeles, CA: n.p., 1944), 47.

9. Ibid., 54.

10. Report, 29 April 1900, Bell to Adjutant General, Department of Northern Luzon, quoted in Linn, *The Philippine War*, 199.

11. Ibid. See also footnote 4 on the term "insurrection."

12. Reprinted in section II.

13. See Robert D. Ramsey III, The Long War Series Occasional Paper 24: *Savage Wars of Peace: Case Studies of Pacification in the Philippines, 1900–1902* (Fort Leavenworth, KS: Combat Studies Institute Press, 2007), 55–58.

14. Report, 31 December 1900, Bell to Adjutant General, quoted in Gates, 214.

15. Ibid., 214–215.

16. Ibid., 215.

17. See Ramsey, 59–63.

18. Report, 17 May 1901, Bell to Adjutant General, US Army, quoted in Glenn A. May, *Battle for Batangas: A Philippine Province at War* (New Haven, CT: Yale University Press, 1991), 247.

19. Linn, *The U.S. Army and Counterinsurgency*, 59.

20. Diary entry, 29 November 1901, Bernard Moses, quoted in May, 248.

21. May, 248.

22. For a brief overview of the 3d Separate Brigade operations, see Ramsey, 95–102. For additional information, see Gates, 256–263; Linn, *Philippine War*, 300–305; Linn, *The U.S. Army and Counterinsurgency*, 152–161; May, 242–269.

23. Gates, 259.

24. Telegram, Brigadier General Bell to Major General Wheaton, 27 December 1901, in US Congress, Senate, *Affairs in the Philippine Islands. Hearings before the Committee on the Philippines of the United States Senate* (Senate Document 331, part 2, 57th Congress, 1st Session, 1902), 1690–1692.

25. John R.M. Taylor, *The Philippine Insurrection Against the United States: A Compilation of Documents with Notes and Introduction, Volume II, May 1, 1898 to July 4, 1902*, 26. This galley proof of an unpublished War Department manuscript is in *History of the Philippine Insurrection against the United States, 1899–1903: and documents relating to the War Department project for publishing the history* (Washington, DC: National Archives, 1968), roll 9.

26. Telegram, Brigadier General Bell to Adjutant-General, Department North Philippine, 11 February 1902 in US Congress, Senate, *Affairs in the Philippine Islands. Hearings before the Committee on the Philippines of the United States Senate* (Senate Document 331, part 3, 57th Congress, 1st Session, 1902), 1717–1718.

27. War Department, *Annual Report of Major General Adna R. Chaffee, United States Army, Commanding the Division of the Philippines, September 30, 1902* (Manila, PI, 1902), 12.

28. Gates, 288.

29. Linn, *The U.S. Army and Counterinsurgency*, 165.

30. Reprinted in section I.

31. Gates, 288.

32. Bell to Senator Albert Beveridge, 16 August 1902, quoted in May, 284.

33. Bell to Secretary of War Root, 6 December 1902, quoted in May, 284.

34. Root to Bell, 3 February 1903, quoted in May, 284.

35. For an overview of Bell's military career, see http://www.army.mil/cmh-pg/books/cg%26csa/Bell-JF.htm (accessed 4 October 2007).

36. Field Marshal Earl Wavell, 1930, lecture to officers at Aldershop. Quoted in Peter G. Tsouras, *Warrior's Words: A Quotation Book, From Sesostris III to Schwarzkopf, 1886 BC to AD 1991* (London: Arms & Armour Press, 1992), 202.

37. Birtle, 101.

38. Gates, 263.

Section I

Bell's Telegraphic Circulars and General Orders*

Telegraphic Circulars and General Orders Regulating Campaign Against Insurgents and Proclamations and Circular Letters Relating to Reconstructions after Close of War in the Provinces of Batangas, Laguna and Mindoro, Philippines Islands. Issued by Brigadier General J. Franklin Bell, US Army, 1 December 1902.

Telegraphic Circulars and General Orders,

Regulating Campaign Against Insurgents and

Proclamations and Circular Letters,

Relating to Reconstruction after Close of War in the Provinces of

BATANGAS, LAGUNA and MINDORO,
PHILIPPINE ISLANDS.

Issued by

Brigadier General J. Franklin Bell, U.S. Army,
COMMANDING BRIGADE,

FROM DECEMBER 1ST, 1901, TO DECEMBER 1ST, 1902,
COMPILED BY

Captain M.F. Davis, 1st U.S. Cavalry,
ADJUTANT GENERAL,

WITH AN APPENDIX CONTAINING

Telegrams of Thanks and Congratulations

FROM

THE PRESIDENT

AND FROM THE

DIVISION, DEPARTMENT AND BRIGADE COMMANDERS.

HEADQUARTERS THIRD SEPARATE BRIGADE,
Batangas, Batangas Province, P.I.,
DECEMBER 1st, 1902.

INDEX TO TELEGRAPHIC CIRCULARS.

-----o-----

D

F

G

H

I

Q

R

S

T

EXPLANATION.

Since the war ended in this Brigade, requests have been received from a large percentage of the officers (who served therein during the last campaign) for copies of Telegraphic Circulars, etc., issued for the purpose of regulating military operations. A number of similar requests have also been received from persons outside of the Brigade.

Very few surplus copies were originally made and these requests could not be complied with, but, as they continued to come, I undertook the preparation of this compilation in order to at least comply with the requests of those who took part in the campaign.

With several exceptions, the following Telegraphic Circulars, General Orders, Proclamations, Circular Letters and Telegrams were originally dictated to a stenographer, and the transcribed notes of most of them carefully corrected and revised by General Bell. But, in transmitting them by wire and in making a mimeographic stencil for reproducing mail copies, a number of errors occurred which were never corrected because of lack of time and opportunity and because they were generally unimportant. Most of them were typographical, but there were some inadvertent omissions and substitutions (of erroneous words) by stenographers, type writers and operators.

It was found by experience also that some of the explanations and provisions contained therein were not sufficiently comprehensive and explicit to preclude the forming of erroneous impressions by persons unacquainted with the local conditions and precedents bearing upon the subject referred to.

Though there have been no material changes in their contents as originally issued, the proof sheets of this pamphlet have been carefully revised by General Bell, for the purpose of correcting the errors and deficiencies above mentioned, and it is believed that its contents will be found substantially correct.

Respectfully,

MILTON F. DAVIS,
Captain, 1st Cavalry,
Adjutant General.

BATANGAS, BATANGAS PROV., P.I.,
DECEMBER 1ST, 1902.

INTRODUCTION.

-----0-----

On December 1, 1901, all the Officers stationed at Batangas, Batangas Province, P.I., called on General Bell in a body. Chairs were brought into the room, and after the Officers were seated General Bell addressed to them the following remarks, which were taken down by two stenographers:—M.F.D.

Gentlemen:—I presume, as is natural, you would like to know just why I have been sent here and what policy I expect to pursue and enforce. I have something to say to you on this subject and am very glad to meet all of you today and to have this opportunity of explaining my views and purposes. I am very well acquainted with the difficulties you have had to contend with, and clearly understand that I shall need not only loyalty to my views and purposes, but also your cordial and energetic co-operation to succeed in the task that has been assigned me. I have been sent here with instructions to put an end to insurrection and re-establish peace in the shortest time practicable. As I am well aware that American officers and soldiers have an individuality and opinions of their own, and can always co-operate with much greater zeal, cordiality, energy and satisfaction when they feel that their Commanding General's views are correct, just and best calculated to accomplish our purpose, it is natural that I should want your views to coincide with mine. I shall therefore take pains to explain my views to you at some length, in the hope that you may become convinced that they are sound and reasonable.

The average American officer and soldier is kind-hearted and sympathetic, and, unless he has been in these Islands sufficiently long to have graduated from all the various schools of experience, it is very difficult for him to give thoroughly loyal and unflinching support to a policy which appears to be inconsistent with his kind and sympathetic feeling toward the ignorant and misguided people of these Islands. Therefore, in the first place, I want to ask you not to conclude that because I expect to radically change the policy which has heretofore been pursued, that I disapprove or am inclined to criticise that policy. I am not. Our general policy has heretofore been one of great benevolence and forbearance, a policy of attraction and conciliation, and I have always sympathized with and vigorously upheld this policy because I think it right in principle. I am sorry to have to acknowledge, however, that in a number of instances this policy has not been as successful or efficient as I had hoped it might always be. In order to give you a clearer comprehension of my present convictions, I shall now review some of the details of our past policy.

All of you who were here in the early days will doubtless recall that before the first Peace Commission arrived in these Islands no definite policy had ever been announced. Except in the city of Manila, the government throughout the Islands was in the hands of insurgents. As we had not come for the purpose of fighting Filipinos, we all had instructions to be kind, considerate and just to them, and our natural sympathy and kindly feeling for them made that policy agreeable to us. But unfortunately, from the very beginning, the natives entirely misunderstood this policy and attributed it to fear and weakness. They became very arrogant, conceited and aggressive. Those of you who were in the city of Manila when it was practically beseiged by insurgents, will remember that they taunted us with being cowards and were exceedingly anxious, to all appearances, to try conclusions with us. By January of 1899 they had become so bold and certain of their comparative strength that feeling and enthusiasm on their part ran high and they tried in every conceivable manner to provoke us into making an attack upon them.

A conviction began to gain ground in the army, first among the soldiers, who came in more intimate contact with the people, then among the officers, that our policy was an error and that sooner or later we would be compelled to give the Filipino army a sound thrashing in order to inspire it with some sense and cause the people to realize that they were trifling with a power far greater than they had any conception of. It soon became perfectly apparent to every one that war had to come, and when it was finally precipitated it came with a rush. The army, stung to the quick by taunting insults of arrogant, conceited, presumptions and ungrateful enemies, went at them with such vigor that they were swept like chaff out of our way. Then with a full realization of their utter weakness and folly, benevolence and sympathy succeeded excitement, and, if anything, greater consideration was shown them than ever before, in the vain hope that after their one drastic lesson they would come to their senses and see the futility of prolonging an unequal struggle. In those days, having no prisons, all prisoners captured were speedily liberated. We captured, searched and turned them loose minus arms but plus rations and advice. We frequently received instructions to turn them loose on the battle field after disarming them. I have thus liberated many, some of whom promptly returned to their army and were captured over again. I have captured letters written to insurgents by apparently peaceful residents of towns we were occupying who had pretended to be our best friends. These letters gave full and complete information of our movements and expressed the utmost sympathy for the cause. I would show such letters to the individuals who wrote them, advise them sarcastically to hereafter be more cautious and transact such business by word of mouth, and then admonish them to go and sin no more.

In the Province of Pampanga this policy of benevolence and consideration was entirely efficacious, but I know of no other case in which it succeeded in accomplishing the desired result. But, as I have previously stated, I believe in that policy and always continued to practice it until it became clearly demonstrated that a change was necessary in special localities.

We all soon saw that we would have to commence to imprison captured insurgents and the disloyal element of the population, and that we would have to punish war rebels and war traitors. As long as the benevolent and conciliatory policy succeeded, I advocated a strict adherence to it, but my experience finally convinced me that it alone could not be efficacious in dealing with Tagalos. In fact I think that we have all had sufficient experience to conclude that this policy cannot work with them without modification. They are unquestionably the smartest and best educated of all the tribes in the Philippines Islands, but at the same time they are the most cunning, unscrupulous and conscienceless. They are the most agreeable and attractive, but the most enamoured with independence and license which they mistake for liberty.

Batangas is the very heart of the Tagalo region. Cavite is the cradle of insurrection and the birthplace of many of the political and military leaders. Laguna and Tayabas are but little less addicted to insurrection than the other two. Batangas is the hub of this Brigade. The insurrection has been more vigorously and numerously sustained here, I think, than elsewhere, because Batangas, being richer, has contributed more members to foreign juntas than have the other provinces. These leaders advise their families and friends here to continue the struggle.

But, notwithstanding their advice, the people of BATANGAS can have peace whenever they want it, and it should be our mission to make them want it as soon as we can by legitimate methods.

It is not possible to convince these irreconcilable and unsophisticated people by kindness and benevolence alone that you are right and they are wrong, nor could you likewise convince the ignorant *tao* that what you advise him to do is best and what his *principale* orders him to do is wrong, because the only argument the majority of either class can understand and appreciate is one of physical force.

To successfully deal with the common people, the head men, the leaders, the *principales* are the ones we need to influence. The common *hombre* is dominated body and soul by his master, the *principale*. He is simply a blind tool, a poor down-trodden ignoramus, who does not know what is good for him and cannot believe an American. We cannot appear to him direct. It is impossible. You can no more influence him by benevolent persuasion than you can fly. He is going to do whatever he is told to do by his master or his leaders, because he is incapable of doing anything else.

Therefore, to succeed in our purpose, we must make it to the interest of his leaders to order and counsel him to do that which we want him to do. To bring this about we must make the *principale* the object of our especial study and effort.

In order to carry such a policy to a successful issue it will, in all probability, be generally necessary to adopt drastic measures, but it is not necessary to be harsh, humiliating or overbearing in manner to enforce drastic measures. If you can persist in maintaining a firm and relentless policy with the manner of a Chesterfield, so much the better.

Be considerate and courteous in manner, but firm and relentless in action. Say little, and let acts, not words, convey your meaning. Words from us count for nothing. The more an officer talks the less they think he is going to do. The more he does and the less he says the more apprehensive they become while waiting for what is to happen next. Except when necessary to give due warning, do not tell them what you are going to do, but do it. Above all things do not threaten. Threats are invariably interpreted as a sign of weakness. When necessary to give warning, tell them in a mild and dispassionate way what is forbidden and what will be the consequence of disobedience. The more dispassionate your language, the more cool and collected your manner, the freer from excitement and calmer your tone of voice, the more influence your words will have. But they very soon judge by acts, not words, and this fact should never be forgotten.

I hardly think it necessary to caution those of you who have been in these Islands as much as two years that these people are past masters in the art of deception; that you cannot afford to believe what they say about their relations with the insurrection unless it be backed up by some act which has so committed them to the side of Americans as to greatly antagonize insurgents. When a native has done something of that kind, he can be trusted not to deceive you for the benefit of insurgents, but when, without having committed an open act of friendship for Americans, he comes with profuse professions of friendship and offers to do all he can for you, keep an eye to his motives and watch his actions closely. Whenever he is the first to offer you a house, a bed or other necessity, with profuse protestations of friendship and abuse of insurgents, you should not go to sleep and cease efforts to fathom his real sentiments. Such conduct is frequently an indication of a desire to throw you off your guard and thus enable the schemer to aid your enemies in safety.

I beg you will not think me over suspicious. I do not like suspicious people; I very much dislike those who base ordinary actions upon suspicion; such conduct is very repugnant to us all, but, gentlemen, we are here to conduct war, and, under such circumstances as surround us, we cannot do it successfully without some times acting on suspicion as a necessary precaution.

I have learned this sad fact by experience, for I am naturally unsuspicious. I have frequently let men go and greatly regretted it afterwards when I plainly saw that I ought to have held them a reasonable time for investigation and for hunting evidence against them. I have released men found on the battle field because they told me a plausible story, had no uniform on and because no evidence was at hand showing that they were insurgents. In some cases I subsequently learned that I had released important officers, and when too late I recognized that I had been foolishly sympathetic and lenient. It is very disagreeable to hold natives on suspicion, I even grant that it *seems* unfair and unjust, but, under such circumstances as surround us, it is unquestionably a military necessity and therefore in accordance with the laws of war.

In the Province of Pangasinan, which has always been celebrated for disorder and ladronism, the organized insurrection broke up. Insurgents deserting with their arms, scattered into small bands, and the province was soon at the mercy of a horde of armed cut-throats and robbers. The people became so terrorized they did not dare to help us. Anyone suspected of sympathy or friendship for Americans was promptly assassinated. We could get no information and could accomplish nothing. There was no organized insurrection, but those who possessed the guns were living in the towns by day and raiding the countryside by night. The necessity for garrisoning every town, in order to give protection to those peaceably inclined, soon became apparent. The troops were obtained and the towns were garrisoned. When the people saw we were able to protect them they began to help us, and through persistent efforts in detecting, arresting and confining the scheming, murdering, unscrupulous leaders and ladrones among the people, and through running down and capturing the arms, the province became very tranquil and peace reigned supreme. This was not accomplished, however, without having to do many disagreeable things. At one time more heartless murderers and political assassins had been convicted and hung in that province than in all the rest of the Islands put together. One day, referring to necessary executions, the Division Commander told me, with much concern, that circumstances had forced him to approve more death sentences, he thought, than any one man who ever lived; that such a thing was keenly distressing to him, but that he could see no possible way to avoid it and do his duty.

I was ordered from Pangasinan to Manila, at that time the hot-bed of insurgent intrigue, their base of supply and a safe haven of rest and recuperation for insurgents who were worn out and sick from continuous pursuit in the provinces. I was required by the Division Commander to institute a severe and drastic policy there for the purpose of ridding the city of insurgents, schemers, sympathizers, aiders and abetters. I have never done any duty in my life which was quite so disagreeable, but after six months of such a policy the city was completely changed in political attitude. When I left there I do not believe there was an active insurgent in it and inactive sympathizers were afraid to operate. Just before my departure some active insurgents from the provinces arrived in Manila for rest and recuperation. No former friend or sympathizer could be found who dared to give them food or shelter, and they were finally forced to voluntarily surrender to the Provost Marshal General, and when they did so they confessed they had surrendered because they had no place to live and nothing to eat.

All this was accomplished by a determined and persistent effort to ferret out and punish the guilty, who were held in prison with relentless firmness.

It will unquestionably be necessary for us to adopt in this Brigade a policy similar to that which was enforced in the Province of Pangasinan and in the City of Manila. We owe the pacific people protection and must adopt some way of demonstrating our ability to give it. We must then show our intention to punish insurgents and those who aid and assist them. In doing this we will unquestionably be required, by a sense of duty, to do much that is disagreeable. But after all armed insurgents are forced to submit to constituted authority and peaceful conditions are re-established within the Brigade, we can then be benevolent and generous again and convince the people that we are their real friends. Without first whipping them and convincing them that we are able to accomplish our purposes by force if necessary, we can never gain their friendship, because otherwise we can never command their respect.

In connection with the enforcement of such a policy, I want to mention certain serious difficulties I have encountered in the past which can easily be avoided: The lack of information concerning prisoners of war has always been a source of much embarrassment. Though it may be necessary to confine prisoners on suspicion and may not be possible to investigate their cases promptly, a record can and should be kept by the commanding officer of every station, which should show, concerning every prisoner, his full name, town and barrio in which he lives, date of arrest, by whom arrested, and for what arrested. In case arrested on suspicion of what he is suspected should always be stated in full. All these things are absolutely essential in making subsequent disposition of prisoners. A permanent record must be kept of every prisoner, and when he ceases to be a prisoner the disposition made of him should be noted. Whenever released the date thereof and by whose order the action was taken should be shown. I have known some officers who merely scratched a prisoner's name from the record when releasing him. This is wrong. Full and complete information concerning every prisoner should be retained in the permanent record so it may be available for future reference. It is especially necessary and desirable to give in a column of remarks as full and complete a political history of each prisoner as possible.

I expect to have temporary prisons prepared in all towns as soon as possible. The lack of adequate facilities for confining prisoners has been one of the greatest drawbacks to our success in the past. I am aware that it will be very difficult to provide adequate facilities in most towns for confining many prisoners, but now that the dry, cool season is coming on they can be confined in sheds inside of stockades. Our leniency or failure to hold or punish them has encouraged ignorant people to continue the struggle. They can only understand restraint which is imposed by force, and in the absence thereof they continue to do as they prefer. I promise that each commanding officer shall have facilities for confining prisoners, and, without exceptional reasons, no prisoner shall be released until after the officer who captured and confined him has been consulted. It may become apparent that the release of certain prisoners will best serve our purpose, but no prisoner shall be released whose presence in his accustomed haunts or whose influence would be embarrassing to the operations of the officer who arrested him. Except in the clearest cases of wrong identity or evident error, prisoners of war will not be released until it is shown that their release will serve the interests of the government.

I have a personal prejudice against burning for the reason that I never thought it did much good. On the contrary it has appeared to me that it did more harm than good in most cases. I recognize the impossibility, however, of depriving insurgents of shelter in the mountains without destroying the shelter which is there. With reference to houses and other shelter used as *cuartels* there, I shall subordinate my preference and scruples to the judgement of commanding officers as to what may be necessary. Fortunately there are few private houses there and these are small grass and nipa shacks.

We have only one purpose, and that is to force the insurgents and those in active sympathy with them to want peace. In accomplishing this we must pay particular attention to the attitude of *principales* who live in towns under our protection and are the eyes and ears and business agents of insurgents outside. These are the people we most need to investigate. We must get evidence of their complicity and keep them in prison until they are tired of helping to maintain the insurrection and ready to work for peace. We must deprive the insurgents of supplies and prevent their getting more. But in order to inflict the least hardship practicable upon the people, we must adopt some means by which we can afford protection to those who really desire to be peaceful. We must garrison every town, and I shall secure sufficient additional troops to do this as soon as possible. It will do little good to chase our troops around the country hunting insurgents until we have chased the spies and unarmed pickets out of the towns and barrios. We will simply wear out our men, and the insurgents, well advised in ample time, will continue to avoid us by hiding and make merry over our inability to find them. I presume here, as elsewhere, they have a barrio *hombre* continually stationed on every prominent height who gives them ample warning of approaching troops.

We have been through all of this up north where I have just come from. There every pueblo, barrio and sitio was well organized by the *Katipunans* [members of the Filipino Secret Society]. At first it was impossible to get any information, but by patience and perseverance we finally learned their system, completely broke up their secret organizations in the towns and barrios, and then the insurgents had to surrender. We hope to pursue the same policy here. We soon found we could not get near insurgents living in the mountains by means of movements in the day time. When we learned the paths and trails sufficiently well, we moved only at night, avoiding the barbios and barking dogs.

In the Provinces of Ilocos Norte and Sur some of the people living in the foot hills and mountains and localities distant from the pueblos, wearying of the oppressive exactions of insurgents, moved into the towns. Surprising as it may possibly seem to you, in nearly every town in Ilocos Norte the people, tiring of the insurrection and wishing to protect themselves against the oppressions of insurgent foraging parties, maurauding by night, built bamboo fences around the outskirts of their towns. It is hard to believe that they can build a stockade fence of bamboo from 12 to

14 miles in length in less than a week, but nevertheless it is a fact. When I first saw these fences it seemed to me they could do little good, but the tops of the bamboo poles were sharpened and it was practically impossible to get over them or cut a hole through the fence without making so much noise as to attract attention. They turned the entire population out to work. Some dug the ditches, some cut and sharpened bamboo poles and others set them up in the ditches. When the fences were built the people moved inside and went out only in the daytime. Few gates were left and municipal police guarded these by night. Through this voluntary assistance, we were soon able to starve the insurgents out, as they no longer had their supply organization, for knowing that our troops were covering the country at night their secret agents and spies dare not go out with food.

We found that much of the money paid the people by the government was divided with insurgents, and I presume the same condition is existing here. I shall ask the government to suspend the payment of rents for the present and also to close the ports to prevent insurgents from bringing supplies from the outside.

As many poor people are engaged in furnishing *sacati*, wood and other supplies to the troops, I think it best to pay them. But if, after our policy is changed, they should refuse to work for pay, it is almost certain that they are intimidated by someone. To combat such a move, we will have to arrest the *principales* and local officials and make them get the supplies as prisoners of war unless they are willing to induce the common people to furnish them as usual. When an ignorant *hombre* thus suddenly changes his attitude there can be no doubt he does it because he is ordered to do so.

Assassination in broad daylight and at other times must stop. We must adopt such measures as will make the life of an *Americanista* safer than that of any insurgent in this Brigade. We must demonstrate to those who would be friendly our ability to protect them.

I have requested of General Chaffee 300 copies of G.O. 100, and when received a copy will be furnished to every officer in the Brigade. We shall hereafter conduct war in accordance with that order, and I shall confer upon each officer authority to do any reasonable and just thing which is authorized by that order. It authorizes executing prisoners of war, without trial, in retaliation against assassination, but inasmuch as I do not wish to place this heavy burden of responsibility upon other shoulders than my own, I shall forbid such executions without my authority.

When we make a radical and drastic change of policy by adopting as our guide G.O. 100, it is very probable that great resentment will at first be aroused among the people, and they may at once begin a policy of lawless assassination of American soldiers and civilians, *Americanistas* and native employees, necessitating this severe measure of retaliation. I shall probably apply some other remedial action in Tanauan and Bauan where *Americanistas* have so recently been assassinated in public places in broad daylight, as before adopting such a radical measure I think fairness demands due warning.

It is impossible to announce a general policy equally applicable to all conditions, but the basis of my policy will be to require respect for the American flag and submission to constituted authority. To do this it is not necessary for any one to conduct himself in an ungentlemanly manner, but he must be quick and firm. But whenever one becomes angered and excited it is better to postpone action, to sleep on the matter and act next day. If absolutely essential to act more promptly let anger be controlled and action be moderate but firm.

I presume there are a few people in the Brigade who have rendered Americans such service as to have aroused the bitter resentment of insurgents and subjected their lives to danger. I shall ask that especial efforts be made to protect these people against assassination. They should also be protected from misrepresentation by revengeful sympathizers with insurrection. Be on the watch for false denunciation and intrigues against them. Natives frequently forge letters implicating our best friends and drop them where they will be found by us. Be cautious and investigate carefully before any man is arrested who has been serving us. The revengeful enemy apparently never forgets and frequently abides his time and waits until all the officers who are acquainted with the character and services of friendly natives are ordered away. Then when a new garrison arrives some insurgent will worm himself into the confidence of the new commanding officer for the sole purpose of getting even with those who have really helped us in the past. In order to preclude the possibility of this, every commanding officer ordered away should, before leaving, write a report of the services that such men have rendered and leave it with his successor, sending a copy thereof to these Headquarters. We must avoid, if possible, arresting men who have rendered us friendly services in the past and those who would like to serve us if they felt that we could give them proper protection.

So far as insurgents are concerned, whenever captured or arrested I shall want them held. Turn none of them loose without good reason. If an individual insurgent soldier come in and surrender with a gun, accept his surrender and turn him loose to encourage others to do likewise, but if they come to surrender without guns confine them in prison and keep them there until the guns are forthcoming. We want guns much worse than we want insurgents, and if they should find that they could surrender and obtain liberty without surrendering their arms we would obtain mighty few. When we get all the arms there will be no more insurrection.

I do not want to be understood as advocating any policy which involves unauthorized methods as a means of extracting information. Information so obtained is generally worthless. It sometimes results in getting a gun but seldom leads to important results. We want to accomplish our purpose without resorting to any methods that are liable to demoralize our men and that always do more harm than good.

Prisoners in need of prison discipline may be confined a limited time in dark cells, provided they and the cells are healthy, or be placed in solitary confinement on bread and water for limited periods of time. But doctors should regularly examine them with a view to guarding against doing any permanent injury.

If you have evidence that the officials of any town are concealing information or sending out same to the enemy, they should be tried or properly disciplined. As subjects of the United States these men all owe allegiance to the government, but as public officials who have taken an oath to be loyal and well and faithfully perform their duties, they are under an additional obligation to render loyal service.

I presume it will seem to your judgment, as it does to mine, impossible for a political assassination to occur in any town, in broad daylight, in public places, without every local official and *principale* knowing who did it within 24 hours. If they do not, they can easily find out. Local officials who do not apprehend such assassins, or at least give full information as to their identity to commanding officers, should be arrested and held responsible for neglect of duty.

I have never known an insurgent officer to order a *presidente* to build a bridge or do something else, that it was not promptly done. I have frequently known *presidentes* to make many promises but find it impossible to conclude any necessary public work ordered by commanding officers. To correct such conditions it will only be necessary to use a bit of determination and firmness. Confine the delinquent official in order to teach him you mean what you say and you will doubtless have little trouble in the future.

By cruel ontrages and inhuman expedients, insurgents have created a reign of terror in these Islands which intimidates the people against giving us any assistance, but by legitimate means we must produce sufficient fear of *our* power to at least prevent their helping insurgents. We cannot resort to assassination for this purpose as they do, but by retaliation we can and must render the life of every friendly native and American at least as safe as that of an insurgent anywhere. I shall certainly do all that can be accomplished by legitimate means in this direction. It is my purpose, by giving them proper protection, to turn the inhabitants against the insurrection and secure their earnest and loyal assistance in efforts to re-establish peace. This was accomplished in the north and I believe it can be accomplished here, notwithstanding these people are all Tagalos.

As soon as I have studied the situation a few days, I shall begin the issuance of definite written instructions.

TELEGRAPHIC CIRCULARS.

NO. 1.

DECEMBER 6th, 1901.

TO ALL STATION COMMANDERS:

It is my purpose to send in circular form by wire a number of instructions pertaining to the policy to be pursued in the campaign in this Brigade; copies by mail will follow. It is important that these copies be kept on a separate file to facilitate transference to all successors in case of change of station. In such contingencies these files will, without fail, be turned over to successors and their receipts taken therefor. There will likewise be entered in this file any general authority sent to an individual station commander to pursue any particular policy with reference to his station or district. I hope to visit every station in the Brigade as soon as practicable and will inspect this file of instructions to ascertain if it is complete. The Brigade inspector will be required to do likewise. All station commanders will improvise a file for filing these instructions separately, and will, in addition, have them entered in station records or company books where only one company is present and no post files are kept. Any answer sent to telegram signed by me personally may be addressed to me direct.

J.F. BELL.

NO. 2.

DECEMBER 8th, 1901.

TO ALL STATION COMMANDERS:

In order to put an end to enforced contributions, now levied by insurgents upon the inhabitants of sparsely settled and outlying barrios and districts, by means of intimidation and assassination, commanding officers of all towns now existing in the provinces of Batangas and Laguna, including those at which no garrison is stationed at present, will immediately specify and establish plainly marked limits surrounding each town bounding a zone within which it may be practicable, with an average sized garrison, to exercise efficient supervision over and furnish protection to inhabitants (who desire to be peaceful) against the depredations of armed insurgents. These limits may include the barrios which exist sufficiently near the town to be given protection and supervision by the garrison, and should include some ground on which live stock can graze, but so situated that it can be patrolled and watched. All ungarrisoned towns will be garrisoned as soon as troops become available.

Commanding officers will also see that orders are at once given and distributed to all the inhabitants within the jurisdiction of towns over which they exercise supervision, informing them of the danger of remaining outside of these limits and that unless they move by December 25th from outlying barrios and districts with all their movable food supplies, including rice, palay, chickens, live stock, etc., to within the limits of the zone established at their own or nearest town, their property (found outside of said zone at said date) will become liable to confiscation or destruction. The people will be permitted to move houses from outlying districts should they desire to do so, to construct temporary shelter for themselves on any vacant land without compensation to the owner, and no owner will be permitted to deprive them of the privilege of doing so.

In the discretion of commanding officers the prices of necessities of existence may also be regulated in the interest of those thus seeking protection.

As soon as peaceful conditions have been re-established in the Brigade these persons will be encouraged to return to their homes and such assistance be rendered them as may be found practicable.

J.F. BELL.

NO. 3.

DECEMBER 9th, 1901.

TO ALL STATION COMMANDERS:

A general conviction, which the Brigade Commander shares, appears to exist that the insurrection in this Brigade continues because the greater part of the people, especially the wealthy ones, pretend to desire, but in reality do not want peace. That when all really want peace we can have it promptly. Under such circumstances it is clearly indicated that a policy should be adopted that will as soon as possible make the people want peace and want it badly.

It is an inevitable and deplorable consequence of war that the innocent must generally suffer with the guilty, for when inflicting merited punishment upon a guilty class it is unfortunately at times impossible to avoid the doing of damage to some who do not individually deserve it. Military necessity frequently precludes the possibility of making just discriminations. This is regretable, but it should be borne in mind that the greatest good to the greatest number can best be brought about by putting a prompt end to insurrection. A short and severe war creates in the aggregate less loss and suffering than benevolent war indefinitely prolonged. For reasons here indicated which are well known to all, and chief of which is the delay and difficulty in ascertaining the exact truth, it will be impossible to wage war efficiently and at the same time to do abstract justice in operations unquestionably essential to putting down an insurrection which has long continued in the territory of this Brigade.

Natural and commendable sympathy for suffering and loss and for those with whom friendly relations may have been maintained, should therefore take a place subordinate to the doing of whatever may be necessary to bring a people, who have as yet not felt the distressing effect of war, to a realizing sense of the advantages of peace.

War in the disturbed portions of this Brigade, and, when manifestly necessary, in those portions supposed to be peaceful or which are under civil government, will be conducted in accordance with the provisions of General Order 100, A.G.O., 1863, which publishes instructions for the government of the armies of the United States in the field. The provisions of this order will be strictly adhered to, but no station commander will put any one to death as a matter of retaliation for assassination under Sections 27, 28, 84, and 148, without obtaining authority from a superior commander, nor will the death penalty be inflicted in any case without similar authority. General Order 100 is now being reprinted at Division Headquarters, and when copies are received they will be distributed. Particular attention is invited to the last paragraph of Section 52, in particular reference to possible repetitions of the Balinguiga [Balangiga] affair.

Commanding officers are urged and enjoined to use their discretion freely in adopting any or all measures of warfare authorized by this order which will contribute in their judgment toward enforcing the policy or accomplishing the purpose above announced.

It is not necessary to seek or wait for authority from these headquarters to do anything or take any action which will contribute to the end in view. It is desired that sub-district commanders accord to subordinate commanders and officers a degree of confidence and latitude in operations similar to that herein conferred upon them. Such restraint and supervision only should be exercised as is dictated by sound discretion, and as may be essential to securing concert of action and co-operation when desirable, adherence to authorized methods, and a uniform policy and harmonious action in working for a common end. Subordinate commanders and young officers of experience should not be restrained or discouraged without excellent reason, but should be encouraged to hunt for, pursue and vigorously operate against armed bodies of insurgents wherever they may be found. Considering the comparative moral of our troops and insurgents and the lack of reliable ammunition and training on the part of the latter, it is not believed there exists any just cause for exceptional caution or apprehension in attacking them boldly. At any rate, under present conditions, legitimate chances should be accepted, as excessive caution will do us incalculable harm. Except when the advantage in position and numbers is overwhelming, on the side of the enemy, our troops should always assume the offensive and advance on and pursue them vigorously. The best defense against these people is to assume a vigorous offensive at once. To retire in the presence of this enemy is generally hazardous and discouraging to our troops.

Nothing herein contained will be so interpreted as to warrant or excuse carelessness or a lack of well known and proper precautions. Though troops should be aggressive, they should be military in methods, and precautions against surprise and ambush should never be neglected.

In addition to maintaing [*sic*] active operations against armed bands of insurgents, persistent and systematic efforts will be made through the use of spies, loyal police, native scouts, intelligence officers, provost marshals and provost courts to discover, apprehend and punish all agents, collectors, organizers, contributers and sympathizers who secretly aid, assist and extend encouragement or comfort to those in arms. Many such persons will unquestionably be found among municipal officials and councils and tenientes or cabezas of barrios.

It is so probable as to amount almost to a certainty that the election of all town officials in the provinces of Batangas and Laguna have been dictated by Malvar or other insurgent leaders and that they would never have been permitted to discharge their functions without molestation had they not continued to be subservient to the will of the insurgent leaders and been acting as their agents or at least have done nothing inconsistent with their interests.* It is perfectly safe and easy for town councils to enact the most violent legislation against the insurrection and, sending copies thereof to the insurgent leaders, to secretly inform them that the legislation was enacted under compulsion of Americans or in order to deceive and lull them to sleep, but that the town officials propose to continue their aid of the insurrection secretly just as heretofore. It can be adopted as a rule without danger of error, that whenever an insurgent sympathizer writes a letter or takes any action under pretense of opposition to the insurrection, that he will immediately secretly convey to the insurgent officials the information that he was compelled to do so or did so to mislead Americans. The loyalty of persons should not be judged by such acts or by words alone, nor should the public enactments of councils in favor of peace and against insurrection be accepted as conclusive proof of the loyalty of town officials.

The only acceptable and convincing evidence of the real sentiments of either individuals or town councils should be such acts publicly performed as must inevitably commit them irrevocably to the side of Americans by arousing the animosity and opposition of the insurgent element. Such acts are reliable evidence, but mere words are worthless. No person should be given credit for loyalty simply because he takes the oath of allegiance or secretly conveys to Americans worthless information and idle rumors which result in nothing. Those who publicly guide our troops to the camps of the enemy, who publicly identify insurgents, who accompany troops in operations against the enemy, who denounce and assist in arresting the secret enemies of the government, who publicly obtain and bring reliable and valuable information to commanding officers, those, in fact, who publicly array themselves against the insurgents and for Americans should be trusted and given credit for loyalty, but no others. No person should be given credit for loyalty solely on account of his having done nothing for or against us so far as known. Neutrality should not be tolerated. Every inhabitant of the Brigade should either be an active friend or be classed as an enemy.

Presidentes and chiefs of police against whom sufficient evidence can be found to convict them before a court of violating their oaths by acting as agents for insurgents, or by aiding, assisting or protecting them in any way, should be arrested and confined, and should ordinarily be tried by Military Commission. Charges should be preferred and forwarded with that in view. Other town officials guilty of similar offenses might be tried by Provost Courts unless their offense be too grave for adequate punishment thereby.

Another dangerous class of enemies are wealthy sympathizers and contributors who, though holding no official position, use all their influence in support of the insurrection, and while enjoying American protection for themselves, their families and property, secretly aid, protect and contribute to insurgents. Chief and most important among this class of disloyal persons are native priests. It may be considered as practically certain that every native priest in the provinces of Batangas and Laguna is a secret enemy of the government and in active sympathy with insurgents. These are absolutely our most dangerous enemies—more dangerous even than armed insurgents—because of their unequalled influence. They should be given no exemption on account of their calling. On the contrary, whenever sufficient evidence is obtainable, they should be brought to trial. Should well founded suspicion rest against them, in the absence of competent evidence, they should be confined and held as a necessary military precaution to preclude further activity or bad influence on their part. The same course should be pursued with all of this class, for to arrest anyone believed to be guilty of giving aid or assistance to the insurrection in any way or of giving food or comfort to the enemies of the government, it is not necessary to wait for sufficient evidence to lead to conviction by a court, but those strongly suspected of complicity with the insurrection may be arrested and confined as a military necessity and may be held as prisoners of war in the discretion of the station commanders until receipt of other orders from higher authority. It will frequently be found impossible to obtain any evidence against persons of influence as long as they are at liberty, but once confined, evidence is easily obtainable.

The apprehension and punishment of one individual of the above mentioned classes (men of wealth and standing and officials) is of greater importance and will exercise greater influence than the punishment of a hundred ignorant *hombres* for whose suffering no *principale* cares a straw. The wealthy and influential and town and insurgent officials are therefore those against whom our most energetic efforts should be directed. The common people amount to nothing. They are merely densely ignorant tools who blindly follow the lead of the *principales*. When guilty they must be arrested and confined in order to put an end to further activity on their part, but whenever it is possible to reach their chief or leader through their testimony they may be promised immunity from trial for such simple offenses as aiding or assisting or being insurgents. They should not be released, however, unless they are willing to demonstrate their loyalty by public participation against their former leaders.

The policy herein indicated need not be applied, should commanding officers by convinced it is inadvisable, in those portions of the Brigade where peaceful conditions have been completely re-established, as in Marinduque for example. Discretion should also be exercised as to the degree of rigor to be employed in its enforcement in those portions of the Brigade where civil government exists and where no organized insurrection or intrigue is discoverable.

Provost Courts cannot operate in the Provinces of Cavite and Tayabas, but any disloyal person escaping from Batangas or Laguna into other provinces of the Brigade may be there arrested by the military authorities and be sent back for trial by military courts in the province from which they escaped. Insurgents or armed ladrones residing in Cavite or Tayabas, and operating across the line in Batangas or Laguna, or other persons living in Cavite or Tayaba who furnish aid or assist the insurgents in any way, or who engage in insurrectionary intrigues or operations, will be arrested and reported to these Headquarters for further instructions. Any station in

Batangas or Laguna at which a Provost Court does not now exist will be reported and an officer recommended as such.

Wherever the constabulary have been organized, cordial co-operation will be extended to and solicited from them. Commanding officers will promptly transmit by wire to other commanding officers any information which may possibly be of assistance to them and are expected to seek co-operation and concert of action from each other whenever such may appear to be desirable.

Additional telegraphic instructions will follow suggesting expedients or policies which are believed to be efficacious in particular contingencies. Acknowledge receipt.

J.F. BELL.

---

*It was subsequently ascertained that this was true and applied to the province of Tayabas as well.

NO. 4.   DECEMBER 11th, 1901.

TO ALL STATION COMMANDERS:

It is understood that municipal police in some of the towns of the provinces of Batangas and Laguna are armed with rifles or carbines. It is not known at these Headquarters by what authority such arms were put in the hands of municipal police, but the Brigade Commander desires that they be taken away from all municipal police except those who have actually fought by the side of Americans or have done other things mentioned in Circular Telegram No. 3, which irrevocably commits them to the side of the Americans by arousing the animosity and opposition of the insurgents.

It is also his wish that hereafter no extra pay be given to any municipal police as a mere matter of form or routine or simply because heretofore it may have been paid without discrimination, pursuant to a system established under other conditions. Quartermasters will obtain the funds as usual, but it will be paid in the discretion of the Commanding Officer to those policemen only who publicly render really valuable service to the government against insurgents.

Wherever arms are taken up under this authority, they will be immediately turned over to those accountable for them, an informal receipt being given, for their protection, to those who have been responsible for them.

J.F. BELL.

NO. 5.

TO ALL STATION COMMANDERS:

The United States Government, disregarding many provocations to do otherwise, has for three years exercised an extraordinary forbearance and patiently adhered to a magnanimous and benevolent policy toward the inhabitants of the territory garrisoned by this Brigade. Notwithstanding this fact, opposition to the government has been persistently continued throughout this entire period by a majority of its inhabitants. The enemy, long realizing their inability to maintain themselves without the unanimous co-operation and support of the entire population, have, in order to keep up their useless struggle, established a reign of terror by resorting to atrocities and expedients which violate the well known laws and usages of war as announced in G.O. 100, A.G.O., 1863, approved and published by order of President Lincoln, for the government of the armies of the United States in the field.

1st. They have accepted local offices from the government and taken the oath of allegiance solely for the purpose of improving their opportunities and facilities for deceiving American officials and treacherously aiding and assisting the cause of the insurrection, in violation of Section 26.

2nd. They have, with bolos and other weapons, killed helpless prisoners and soldiers lying on the ground wholly disabled by wounds which prevented their defending themselves in any way, in violation of Sections 49, 56, 61 and 71.

3rd. In order to confuse their identity and thereby be able the more safely to conduct their skulking operations, they have adopted the uniform of our army and native troops without any plain, striking and uniform mark of distinction of their own, in violation of Section 63.

4th. They have improvised and secreted in the vicinity of roads and trails rudely constructed infernal machines propelling poisoned arrows or darts, in violation of Section 70, thus placing themselves beyond the pale of the laws and usages of war.

5th. Men and squads of men without commission, without being part or portion of the regularly organized hostile army, without sharing continuously in the war, but with intermittent returns to their homes and avocations, and with frequent assumption of the semblance of peaceful pursuits, divesting themselves of the character and appearance of soldiers, have committed hostilities by fighting and making raids of various kinds, after which, concealing their arms, they have returned, posing as peaceful citizens, and secretly lived in the same towns with garrisons of our troops, in violation of Section 82.

6th. Armed prowlers have stolen within the lines of our army to cut telegraph wires and destroy bridges. Armed assassins, designated and controlled by the enemy, have come, disguised as peaceful citizens, into the very presence of our garrisons and have assassinated, in broad daylight in crowded market places, persons unlawfully condemned to death by the enemy for being friendly to or assisting the legitimately organized government—the fear, sympathy or co-operation of the entire population effectually preventing our apprehension and punishment of the assassins. This in violation of Section 84.

7th. The apparently pacific inhabitants of towns occupied by the American army have treacherously risen in arms against it, in violation of Section 85.

8th. A large percentage of the population, though owing allegiance to the American government under the provisions of Section 26, have acted as spies and war traitors, in violation of the provisions of Sections 88, 90 and 92.

9th. A very great number of insurgent officials, soldiers and other aiders and abettors of the insurrection, after voluntarily surrendering and after having been captured, have been pardoned, and released from confinement upon taking the oath of allegiance or given paroles, and have subsequently violated their oaths or paroles without scruple by again entering the service of the insurgent army, or aiding and assisting the same, in violation of Sections 26, 124 and 130.

Against but one of these flagrant violations of the laws of war, namely, murder, has the United States Government ever adjudged or executed the severe penalties authorized by the sections of the law above cited, in the vain hope that, by this exercise of forbearance and generosity, the people might be conciliated and become reconciled to and convinced of the benevolent purposes of the government. Instead of having the desired effect, however, this policy in the provinces of Batangas and Laguna has apparently failed to appeal to even the keenest and most appreciative intellects. On the contrary, it has been interpreted by many as an evidence of weakness and fear, and puffed up by a childish and ignorant conceit over what they are pleased to consider successful resistance of our power, the people have become so arrogant that they look down upon our government and scorn its kindliest efforts at pacification. We consequently find ourselves operating in a thoroughly occupied terrain against the entire population, united in a hopeless struggle, using, conniving at or tolerating barbarous methods which almost reach the limit in outraging the laws and usages of legitimate warfare.

The reckless expedients adopted by the enemy, especially the policy of intimidation and assassination, leave to the Brigade Commander no other means of protecting either the lives of his subordinates, or those of peaceful and friendly citizens, or the interests of his government against the repetition of barbarous outrage, except the enforcement of the penalties authorized by the above cited laws of war, and he has reluctantly concluded it to be absolutely necessary to avail himself of the right of retaliation under the provisions of Sections 59 and 148, whenever the duly and carefully ascertained conditions and circumstances warrant the same under the restrictions prescribed in Section 28.

The Brigade Commander therefore announces for the information of all concerned, that wherever prisoners or unarmed or defenseless Americans or natives friendly to the United States government are murdered or assassinated for political reasons, and this fact can be established, it is his purpose to execute a prisoner of war under the authority contained in Sections 59 and 148. This prisoner of war will be selected by lot from among the officers or prominent citizens held as prisoners of war, and will be chosen when practicable from those who belong to the town where the murder or assassination occurred.

It is also his purpose to severely punish, in the same or a lesser degree, the commission of other acts denounced by the aforementioned articles. In this connection the attention of all American officers is invited to the last paragraph of Section 29 and to the provisions of Section 134. Commanding officers are authorized to enforce the provisions of this latter section wherever they may deem it just and practicable.

J.F. BELL.

NO. 6. DECEMBER 13th, 1901.

TO ALL STATION COMMANDERS:

In the case of armed prowlers and others who cut telegraph wires and destroy bridges within the provisions of Batangas and Laguna, the measures and degree of retaliation will be left to the discretion of sub-district commanders, who, in the measures adopted, will observe the principles announced in Section 28, G.O. 100. In order that these measures may be uniform and consistent in contiguous localities, no station commander will execute any measure of retaliation for this violation of Section 84, G.O. 100, without first having obtained from the sub-district commander, general instructions on the subject.

The following expedients have been tried with success: Wherever the line was cut or bridges were burned in such close proximity to cities or barrios as to raise a strong presumption that it was done by the hostile element of those places, a number of houses of that place, proportioned to the damage done, were burned. Another expedient which has been very efficacious elsewhere has been numbering each telegraph pole and assigning those within the jurisdiction of any town or barrio to the *presidente* or *cabeza* of the said town or barrio for special care and supervision, with instructions to assign a native of the town or barrio to each pole, whose duty it should be to replace it immediately if destroyed.

Inasmuch as there is no doubt that, in the provinces of Batangas and Laguna, the municipal officials almost without exception are hostile to us, it is deemed expedient that any destruction of property in retaliation for damage to telegraph lines or bridges should include the houses of the said officials, exception being made only in the case of those officials who have already demonstrated their loyalty by acts at the time the damage is done.

J.F. BELL.

NO. 7.
December 15th, 1901.

TO ALL STATION COMMANDERS:

Though Section 17, G.O. 100, authorizes the starving of unarmed hostile belligerents, as well as armed ones, provided it leads to a speedier subjection of the enemy, it is considered neither justifiable nor desirable to permit any person to starve who has come into towns under our control seeking protection. Although many of these persons can unquestionably be classed as enemies with perfect justice, it is too difficult to discriminate between the hostile and those who really desire peace to inaugurate or permit any policy of starvation under such circumstances. Every proper effort will be made at all times to deprive those in arms in the mountains of food supplies, but in order that those who have assembled in the towns may not be reduced to want it is absolutely essential to confiscate, transport to garrisoned towns and save for future contingencies, whenever possible, every particle of food supply which may be found concealed in the mountains for insurgents or abandoned at a distance from towns.

Therefore, instead of destroying animals and food products, found by troops under such circumstances, commanding officers will make every possible effort to see that such animals and food are brought into the nearest town and kept under control of the military authorities for future use. In accomplishing this, all means of transportation may be seized and every able bodied male impressed and marched under guard to transport said food products into towns.

Though it is recognized that it may be difficult at times to accomplish the above instructions, it is expected that every reasonable effort will be made to do so, even at the expense of time, care and labor, and that no rice or food will be destroyed except where absolutely impracticable to get it to towns. It should not take more than a week to completely clear all outlying districts of food products. Station commanders will begin at once to hunt for and bring in these supplies. Food abandoned may be given to those townspeople who will bring it in, if impossible to get it in for the government.

Storehouses in which to store these products will be taken possession of, or when none are available the *presidente* will be required to build one with labor and material of the town without compensation from the government. These products will be carefully preserved by the garrison for future issue in accordance with a system to be announced hereafter. The rice of persons believed to be disloyal, beyond an amount necessary for themselves and dependents, may be confiscated and preserved for the same purpose.

No rice or food supplies thus seized will be fed to public animals, nor will any of it be consumed by troops except in case of emergency and necessity. None of this food will be issued gratis to well-to-do people who have means and property on which they can raise money to buy it, but when such people have no rice and are unable to purchase it elsewhere, these government stores may be sold in small quantities at a reasonable rate. The money thus accumulated will be used to purchase other rice in Manila to be transported by the government and resold at the same price or issued gratis to paupers.

The utmost care will be taken in registering paupers and the members of their families, in order that frauds may be prevented in the gratuitous issue of food.

In the discretion of sub-district commanders, after consulting station commanders, a uniform scale may be established, regulating the prices that may be charged by merchants for ordinary and necessary food supplies.

Sub-district commanders may also transfer any surplus of government stores from one town to another which needs it worse.

It is the purpose of this order to place the burden of feeding the poor upon the wealthy classes, whose disloyalty has brought on and maintained this war, and upon those who still remain disloyal, especially upon those who are actively sympathizing, contributing to, and otherwise aiding and assisting the insurrection. See provisions of Sections 21, 37, 38 and 156, G.O. 100.

J.F. BELL.

NO. 8. December 17th, 1901.

TO ALL STATION COMMANDERS:

Information has frequently been received at this office relating to movements of insurgents and taken from captured correspondence, without mentioning the date of said movements or of correspondence from which information is taken.

Information given by natives to local officers has also been repeated here, and on investigation the information was found to be weeks or months old.

The attention of all officers is invited to the fact that it is impossible to judge of the value or significance of such information without knowing the date thereof, which is of first importance. The hour should also be given, if practicable, when insurgents were observed moving or in camp in any locality.

J.F. BELL.

NO. 9. December 17th, 1901.

TO ALL STATION COMMANDERS:

Whenever the treasurer of any town is arrested, the commanding officer will immediately designate an officer who will secure the treasurer's books and accounts and take charge of any funds in his possession, giving him an informal receipt therefor for his protection. This action will then be reported to these Headquarters with a statement of amount of money on hand. If the local commanding officer thinks it wise or safe to do so he may nominate another native treasurer and report his name for confirmation by the Brigade Commander.

These instructions will apply in the provinces of Batangas and Laguna only. No municipal treasurer will be arrested in those provinces under civil government without first having obtained authority and instructions from these Headquarters.

J.F. BELL.

NO. 10.   DECEMBER 20th, 1901.

TO ALL STATION COMMANDERS:

Commanding officers in the provinces of Batangas and Laguna will prepare to send out commands on the 26th of December and every day thereafter until January 1st, for the especial purpose of hunting insurgents and disloyal persons and confiscating and bringing into government storehouses all rice and food supplies found within the jurisdiction of their town and outside the zone of protection. Rice found in the possession of families so situated will, if practicable, be moved with them to towns; that found abandoned or apparently stored in mountains or other places for insurgents will be confiscated and brought in for the government.

In accomplishing this, commanding officers are authorized to impress every possible means of transportation, including able bodied males, as burden bearers, and the use of prisoners of war. When large quantities of rice are found so located as to render it possible to transport it to town, a guard will be left over it until sufficient transportation can be secured for moving it. The families of poor people, women and children, of the town, may be notified that they can go out and take for their own use as much of the rice as they can transport.

It is desired that all commanding officers make an especial effort during these six days to accumulate as large a store of rice within the towns as possible, but whenever it is found absolutely impossible to transport it to a point within the protected zone, it will be burned or otherwise destroyed. These rules will apply to all food products.

J.F. BELL.

NO. 11.   DECEMBER 20th, 1901.

TO ALL STATION COMMANDERS:

Hereafter, except by special authority from these Headquarters, no enlisted men of this command, or native or American scouts, or natives or

Americans employed by the military authorities, will be permitted to own or have in their possession any native horses or stock of any description.

If there are any such persons who now own such animals, for which they have bills of sales, commanding officers will see that they dispose of them at once. In case they have no bills of sale, their ownership will be carefully investigated and unless they can clearly prove legitimate title, the animals will be turned into the Quartermaster's Department, be branded "U.S.," and be taken up on the returns.

There may be a few American and native employees whose duty requires them to be mounted and who may have horses for use in their work; there may also be a few natives employed by the government who own and have horses for their family use. Such cases will be reported and explained in detail, requesting authority to retain them, should commanding officers deem it necessary or desirable that they retain them. The Quartermaster's Department will furnish public mounts to others who need them. All stock captured or taken up will at once be turned into the Quartermaster's Department and be taken up and accounted for. After this order has been complied with, individuals mentioned in first paragraph will not be permitted to claim stock so acquired under any circumstances whatever.

J.F. BELL.

NO. 12.

DECEMBER 21st, 1901.

TO ALL STATION COMMANDERS:

Though the Brigade Commander is desirous that officers should be bold and aggressive in their work, and work fearlessly with small parties at night, he desires to remind all of the necessity for unceasing vigilance and for the usual precautions against surprise and ambush.

He again wishes to repeat that ordinarily the best defense can be made by assuming the offensive, that if small parties are caught by an overwhelming force, it is better to stand their ground, if any suitable position whatever can be obtained, than to undertake to retreat in plain view. An orderly retreat might be accomplished when there is ample cover to conceal the movement, or at night, but it is exceedingly hazardous for small parties in the day time to scatter and undertake to retreat individually.

Inasmuch as the change of policy which has recently taken place is calculated to arouse strong resentment on the part of the enemy, all persons should expect greater aggressiveness and activity on their part. For the present, commanding officers should not permit very small detachments of footmen to undertake operations by daylight so far away as to render reinforcement in a reasonable time impossible.

The telegraphic instructions of recent date requiring all cavalry soldiers to wear their revolvers and infantry soldiers to wear their bayonets sharpened when they go about towns, will be strictly enforced. No soldier should be permitted to go beyond the immediate vicinity of the garrison alone under any circumstances.

J.F. BELL.

NO. 13.

December 21st, 1901.

TO ALL STATION COMMANDERS:

On account of the large number of people who have assembled in towns seeking the protection of American troops, and to guard against treachery, all commanding officers in the provinces of Batangas and Laguna, and of those towns in Tayabas where people have so assembled, will notify them, through their proper representatives, that if the people of the town should treacherously arise against the troops, the town will be completely destroyed by fire as a measure of retaliation against such treachery, under the provisions of Section 27 and the last paragraph of Section 52, G.O. 100.

J.F. BELL.

NO. 14.

December 21st, 1901.

TO ALL STATION COMMANDERS:

On and after January 1st, 1902, all traffic on roads or trails outside of the protected zones, for any purpose whatever, all passing of persons or merchandise to and fro between towns will be strictly forbidden by all commanding officers in the towns of Batangas and Laguna. No persons will be permitted to leave the town without a written pass from the commanding officer thereof, said pass to show length of time the said individual has permission to be absent, where permitted to go and for what purpose. If the pass is to go to a neighboring town, the holder will be required to present it to the commanding officer thereof, who will note this fact and the hour on the pass. Unless the holder is back by the expiration of the specified time, arrest and confinement will follow. No pass will be given to any able bodied male for any purpose whatever, except in case of extreme necessity, and no pass will be given an able bodied male to go anywhere to do anything which a woman can do equally well.

An exception will be made in those towns where it may be practicable to permit the people to gather standing crops, under the protection of patrols or detachments of soldiers.

Any able bodied male found by patrols or scouting detachments outside of protected zones without passes will be arrested and confined, or shot if he runs away. No old or feeble man or any woman or child will be shot at pursuant to this rule.

Any merchandise found outside of protected zones after January 1st, 1902, will be confiscated for the government or destroyed.

J.F. BELL.

NO. 15.

December 23rd, 1901.

TO ALL STATION COMMANDERS:

In addition to the provisions of Telegraphic Circular No. 14, the following restrictions upon internal trade and commerce will be enforced throughout the provinces of Batangas and Laguna:

1.   The manufacture of copra is hereby forbidden in these two provinces, until further orders, and commanding officers will see that cocoanuts are preserved as food supplies to guard against anticipated necessities. The cocoanuts of any person found violating the above prohibition will be confiscated by the government and stored for issue to the poor in case of necessity.

2.   Information has been received from Manila that business firms of that city, heretofore engaged in the business of buying country produce in these provinces, have sent large sums of money to their agents with a view of continuing purchases of produce during the period of closed ports and to accumulating them against the day when the ports will again be reopened. Inasmuch as this proceeding would partially defeat the purpose of closing the ports and be a great impediment to the successful issue of military operations, commanding officers will close all establishments conducted by Chinos and others which make a business of purchasing country produce and absolutely prohibit all further commercial transactions on their

part. The manager or managers of any such establishment caught violating this prohibition will be arrested and reported to these Headquarters for further instructions, together with a detailed statement of their offense.

3.   No one will be permitted to purchase rice or food supplies in large quantities for the purpose of speculation or selling at a high figure should food products become scarce.

4.   No rice or food products will be permitted to leave the limits of protected zones except by special permission of the military authorities, which will be given only under such circumstance as will preclude its falling into the hands of insurgents.

J.F. BELL.

NO. 16.   DECEMBER 23rd, 1901.

TO ALL STATION COMMANDERS:

Commanding officers of towns in the provinces of Batangas and Laguna are reminded of the provisions of Telegraphic Circular No. 3, which authorizes them to regulate the prices of food products in case of necessity. They will accordingly keep a close watch on such prices for the purpose of preventing extortion, and if, after regulating them, Chinos and others are found violating said regulations, drastic measures will be used to preclude such violations in the future. There are no persons doing business in these provinces who have not from time to time contributed to the insurrection and thereby rendered themselves liable to suffer the hardships of the war, under the provisions of G.O. 100.

Chinamen especially will be warned against buying up food products for the purpose of securing a monopoly and establishing a high price, and, if they undertake to violate regulations in this regard, commanding officers will require them to sell out at public auction, close up their establishments, and deport them from the Brigade to Manila.

J.F. BELL.

NO. 17.   DECEMBER 23rd, 1901.

TO ALL STATION COMMANDERS:

All commanding officers in the provinces of Batangas and Laguna are warned against beginning to issue food gratuitously until want and privation absolutely necessitates it. Wherever government stores of rice are held it is best to preserve the same until the current supply in the town has been used up at regulated prices, then the government rice may be sold at the same regulated prices to those who are able to buy it. Many of the very poor people who have no food nevertheless have money with which they can buy it, and none should be issued gratuitously until it has been thoroughly determined by a searching investigation that the individuals applying for charity have no means with which to purchase food.

Such persons, with the membership of their families, will be carefully registered and will be issued very limited supplies of food at frequent periods, preferably daily. In issuing rice each adult member of a family will be allowed for the present one chupa per day, and the same amount to each two children. A chupa measure can be found in any retail shop. Great pains will be taken not to unduly pauperize the people, for if they discover any unwise or excessive liberality in the free issue of food, the entire population (excepting the rich and well-to-do) will certainly flock around and claim to be paupers in order to obtain free issues of food. All officers should carefully husband their supplies in anticipation of a period of real want and suffering.

Wherever there are standing crops still ungathered, it is desired that commanding officers give protection to peaceful people in order to enable them to gather their palay. It is also desired that, whenever conditions become favorable for the planting of new food crops, commanding officers likewise give protection, and such assistance as may be practicable, to those who have gathered at towns (seeking our protection) in order that they may re-plant their land.

J.F. BELL.

NO. 18.

DECEMBER 23rd, 1901.

TO ALL STATION COMMANDERS:

Wherever similar action has not already been taken, commanding officers of all garrisoned towns in the provinces of Batangas and Laguna, on the first day of January, 1902, or as soon there after as practicable, will, with the exceptions hereinafter noted, arrest all native municipal officials, including *cabezas* of barrios, leading *principales*, members of police force (who have not fully complied with their duty by actively aiding the Americans and rendering them valuable service) and any other person in the community who is known to be or is strongly suspected of being an active aider or abbettor of the insurrection, or a sympathizer therewith who uses his influence against the American government. Though all such persons will be arrested without distinction, it is especially desirable that no guilty *principales* or prominent persons escape.

Exception may be made of any one of the persons above mentioned who has demonstrated his loyalty by methods mentioned in Telegraphic Circular No. 3, or who has given secret aid and information of value to the commanding officer, but no neutrals will be spared. The secret repetition of idle rumors or information that everybody knows is to be considered valueless.

All persons not so arrested will be given to clearly understand that the time has now come when the principal people of each town have either got to go to prison as suspects or organize and work for peace by notifying insurgents that they will no longer aid or assist them, but will aid the government by denouncing insurgents who secretly enter towns in disguise, by giving to commanding officers all information of insurgent plans and movements that come to their notice, by refusing to contribute any longer either money or food, by assisting in defending the towns against attack, and by doing other things mentioned in Telegraphic Circular No. 3 to demonstrate their loyalty.

It is not intended by this circular to deprive station commanders of discretion, but it is desired that under its provisions they adopt an advanced and stringent policy and maintain it relentlessly.

In case of necessity, commanding officers are authorized to appoint new municipal officials, or, in their discretion, to detail an officer or noncommissioned officer to conduct the affairs of the town. The taxes will be collected as usual and disbursed for the benefit of the pueblo. Whenever an officer is not specially detailed for the purpose, the commanding officer will exercise close supervision over the collection and disbursement of the revenue, the usual taxes at the usual rates being collected in each town. In this connection attention is invited to the provisions of Telegraphic Circular No. 9.

J.F. BELL.

NO. 19. DECEMBER 24th, 1901.

TO ALL STATION COMMANDERS:

In order to make the existing state of war and martial law so inconvenient and unprofitable to the disloyal people that they will earnestly desire and work for the re-establishment of peace and civil government, and for the purpose of throwing the burden of the war upon the disloyal element, pursuant to the provisions of paragraphs 21, 37, 76 and 156, G.O. 100, the following expedients may, in the discretion of sub-district and station commanders, be adopted throughout Batangas and Laguna:

1st.   Until the re-establishment of civil government and the making of provisions thereby for the repair of roads and performance of other public work, the old Spanish law, requiring either fifteen days free labor or three pesos tax in lieu thereof, may be enforced and road work be begun as soon as it is practicable or safe to do so. Station commanders will see that Engineer officers in charge of road construction are furnished free labor, and the money collected pursuant to this provision will be used to purchase rice for those who labor. Wherever no Engineer officer is at work, and there is a piece of road needing repair, station commanders will, when practicable, detail an officer to supervise the repair and put the people to work, and will furnish the officer so detailed with sufficient assistance of soldiers and non-commissioned officers to give protection to and require those working to labor faithfully and intelligently. Where no officer is available, a suitable non-commissioned officer will be detailed in charge of the work. The object of this provision is to give beneficial occupation to the able bodied men concentrated in towns and to compel them to earn food for themselves and families. With this purpose in view, lists will be immediately prepared of all the *principales*, who will have the privilege of either paying three pesos or working, but all poor people (able bodied males) will be required to work in turn, it being undesirable to take money from them. Those who work on the road will be daily supplied, by arrangement with the officer in charge of the work, with sufficient rice for themselves and families from confiscated rice on hand and from that bought with the three peso tax on the well-to-do.

2nd. Cock-fighting, as now conducted in these two provinces, has been a source of very considerable revenue to insurgents and a convenient means of enabling the insurgent element to secretly mingle, impose upon and intrigue with the portion of the people who may prefer to be peaceful. Upon receipt of these orders, all commanding officers will forbid further cock fighting until authority to renew the same is obtained from these headquarters. It is proposed to again tolerate cock-fighting as soon as peace is re-established throughout the Brigade, or whenever satisfactory conditions are re-established in any towns, the privilege may again be tolerated in those towns. Whenever station commanders become satisfied that the sentiment of the town has entirely changed, and the people have arrayed themselves publicly and sincerely against the insurrection, a recommendation to tolerate the renewal of cock-fighting, explaining the conditions and circumstances on which the recommendation is based, will be considered at these headquarters.

3rd. Whenever station commanders are convinced that collections are being made for the benefit of the insurgent cause, in public markets, they are authorized to close the same with the consent and approval of sub-district commanders. Inasmuch, however, as this is the only means some poor and inoffensive people have for gaining a livelihood, this expedient should be resorted to only when it is considered essential to preventing the abuse mentioned. By proper discipline of municipal police, thereby compelling them to do their duty and arrest collectors and other insurgents who enter market places, this expedient ought not to become necessary.

4th. Whenever necessary for the success of field operations, commanding officers of troops are authorized to seize and use, without compensation at present, carabao, ponies and other means of transportation, including the impressment of burden bearers or the use of prisoners of war for the same purpose, pursuant to the provisions of Section 76.

5th. When on active campaign, and troops run out of rations, commanding officers are authorized to levy necessary contributions of food on the inhabitants of hostile sections, and at all times sufficient rice may be obtained to feed burden bearers or prisoners used as such, under provisions of preceding paragraph. Animals seized for temporary use will not ordinarily be fed on palay, but the people may be required to cut and deliver *sacate* for them, without compensation, when troops are in the field.

6th. Until further orders the people of all towns and protected zones will be required to enter their habitations not later than 8 p.m., and to refrain from again appearing upon the street or outside of habitations before the break of day the following morning. Patrols will be frequently sent out in different directions at night and will arrest and confine all persons discovered out and about at night.

All commanding officers will exercise care that no authorized acts or abuses grow out of the enforcement and application of the foregoing provisions. An exception will always be made in the case of those who have demonstrated their loyalty in the manner explained in Telegraphic Circular No. 3. Their lives, families and property will not only be given protection, as far as practicable against insurgents, but will be carefully respected by our troops and great care will be taken in seeing that as little damage is done their interests as is consistent with the success of the government. Whenever it is found that their property has been seized for use by mistake it will be returned to them as soon as the necessities of the government will admit.

The provisions of this circular apply to the provinces of Batangas and Laguna only.

J.F. BELL.

NO. 20.

DECEMBER 24th, 1901.

TO ALL STATION COMMANDERS:

In the discretion of commanding officers the following measures of discipline may be enforced in the provinces of Batangas and Laguna, against disorderly persons and officials:

1st. *Presidentes* and *cabezas* will be required to notify the nearest military commander at once whenever insurgents are discovered to be within the limits of their jurisdiction. For any failure in this regard they will be tried and punished by Provost Court. In addition to this punishment any *presidente* or *cabeza* discovered to be concealing or protecting the enemy or furnishing false information or guides may be impressed as guides themselves and may be marched on foot daily at the head of columns or detachments until they have had a drastic lesson.

2nd. Should the inhabitants of any town fail or refuse to furnish *sacate* or wood, and there be no assignable reason for said failure or refusal apparent to commanding officers, said failure or refusal may, without danger of error, be attributed to the influence or threats of disloyal *principales* or officials. In such a contingency, commanding officers may arrest *principales* and officials believed to be disloyal, and joining them with insurgent officers and prominent and influential persons held as prisoners of war, march them out under guard and require them to cut and deliver *sacate* until they are willing to induce the poor people to furnish it for compensation as usual.

3rd. If there are any local officials who desire to resign and who are serving under compulsion, they should be notified that if they run away or try to evade or neglect such duty, they will be punished by imprisonment. Should any of them try to escape, all neighboring commanding officers will be notified at once to arrest them if found.

4th. Whenever it is ascertained beyond a doubt that guns have been concealed in barrios or on premises of disloyal persons, they will be notified to turn them in within a given time on pain of having the barrio or premises burned in case they fail to do so.

The utmost pains should be taken, however, to be certain that guns have been so hidden before the notification is given.

5th.   All officers will exact respect for the American flag, and for officers and bodies of troops as representatives of the great nation to which they pertain. It has resulted from the lenient policy which the government has heretofore pursued that the people of these islands look down upon the representatives of the government to such an extent as to pass by them and their flag with sullen disdain. Hereafter all natives of this brigade, irrespective of standing, will be required to show that respect which is due from the people to the government of occupation.

6th.   Commanding officers will have all parts of the uniform of American soldiers, found in the possession of natives, not authorized to wear them, seized, and soldiers and native troops caught selling any portion of their uniform should be severely punished.

7th.   Hereafter, whenever sequestration or assassination takes place in towns in broad daylight and in crowded places (as has frequently occurred heretofore), commanding officers will immediately call upon local officials to ascertain and report without delay the names of the assassins with the evidence necessary for their conviction, and to arrest them if possible. If said officials do not know, they can certainly ascertain who such assassins are. If they fail to do so under such circumstances, they should be brought to trial for neglect of duty by Provost Court.

Commanding officers will promptly report to these headquarters all sequestrations and assassinations, detailing facts and circumstances, in order that further instructions may be given.

8th.   The attention of all local officials and others who have been in the habit of furnishing the enemy timely information of the movements of American troops, should be called to the provisions of Sections 90 and 91, G.O. 100, and the attention of all foreigners should likewise be called to the provisions of Section 98.

J.F. BELL.

NO. 21.

DECEMBER 24th, 1901.

TO ALL STATION COMMANDERS:

The primary and most important object of all our operations in this

Brigade is to obtain possession of the arms now in the hands of insurgents and disloyal persons, and incidentally to capture as many insurgents as possible, especially those accused of grave offenses against the laws of war.

1st. As the surrender of individuals (who have not been guilty of assassinations and violations of oaths of allegiance) without procuring all their arms is a matter of very slight importance to us, it is not considered desirable to accept the proffered surrender of any insurgents unless at the same time they surrender all the guns under their control. The following exceptions will be made to the above rule: The surrender of individual soldiers presenting themselves with serviceable guns will be accepted and they will be turned loose, after taking the oath of allegiance. The unconditional surrender of staff officers, collectors and other agents may be accepted, without arms, in case it is believed they have none, but, in such cases, they will be confined and will be retained in confinement until they have rendered valuable service against the insurgents and demonstrated their loyalty in the manner explained in Telegraphic Circular No. 3.

2nd. All surrenders of line officers must likewise be unconditional, and prior to permitting line officers to earn their liberty it must be as correctly ascertained as possible whether they have had any arms under their control, and the securing of these arms must be a condition of their release. The full number of guns that they have had in their possession will be exacted before their release will be favorably considered at these headquarters. Whenever insurgent officers and soldiers are CAPTURED they will, as a rule, be brought to trial by Provost Court for violation of the laws of war by participating in guerrilla warfare, unless they immediately render such valuable service to the government as may be considered sufficient to merit leniency.

3rd. The following rewards will be paid to agents, spies, guides, etc.: To those who either secure insurgent guns or give information and furnish guides which enable detachments of our troops to secure them, thirty (30) pesos for each serviceable gun; to those who capture insurgent officers or give information and guide our troops in such a way as to enable them to capture said officers, five (5) pesos will be paid for every officer captured below the rank of major, and ten (10) pesos for every officer above the rank of captain. For information leading to the capture of general officers, greater rewards, to be agreed upon, may be offered.

4th. No oaths of allegiance will be administered to anyone simply and solely for the purpose of giving them additional security against responsibility for their past conduct. Only those who have demonstrated their loyalty by methods mentioned in Telegraphic Circular No. 3 will be permitted to take the oath of allegiance. It will be refused to all others who apply for it.

Before any insurgent, who has been operating in another jurisdiction than that in which he surrenders, is permitted to take the oath of allegiance and released, the commanding officer at the post at which he surrenders will telegraph to the commanding officer of the town near which he has been operating and ascertain whether there are any charges against him for violations of the laws of war.

The money to pay for guns will be obtained from the Quartermaster's Department; rewards for the capture of officers will be paid from secret service funds.

J.F. BELL.

NO. 22.

DECEMBER 24th, 1901.

TO ALL STATION COMMANDERS:

The purpose of the preceding telegraphic circulars of instruction has been to place the burden of the war on the disloyal and to so discipline them that they will become anxious to aid and assist the government in putting an end to the insurrection and in securing the re-establishment of civil government. Their provisions are based upon the assumption that, with very few exceptions, practically the whole population has been hostile to us at heart. In order to combat such a population, it is necessary to make the state of war insupportable, and there is no more efficacious way of accomplishing this than by keeping the minds of the people in such a state of anxiety and apprehension that living under such conditions will soon become unbearable.

Little should be said; the less said the better. The making of threats which cannot be carried out should especially be carefully guarded against. Let acts, not words, convey intentions. The more an officer does and the less he says about what he is going to do the more apprehensive and anxious will become those who are guilty and who wait for what is next to happen. When it becomes necessary to give warning or publish instructions, it should be done dispassionately, and not in a threatening way.

The main object of the policy being to cause the people to change their minds and to conclude that it is best to help the government to put down this insurrection, a tendency in this direction will be encouraged, and as soon as officers observe that the people have come to their senses, they may modify the rigor of enforcement of this policy so far only as may be necessary to encourage and welcome those who might really and sincerely be desirous of lending assistance.

Officers are again cautioned, however, not to judge or be mislead by words alone. They must rely solely upon acts in order to form a correct judgement of sincerity. The benefit of every doubt should be given to the government.

Those people who have demonstrated their loyalty and sincere desire to assist, by methods mentioned in Telegraphic Circular No. 3, should be spared, and protected as much as possible, in order to make a distinction between them and the disloyal.

Though it is intended and desired that the policy to be enforced shall be as rigid and relentless as it properly can be, until the people have changed their policy and completely turned against the insurgents, the Brigade Commander relies upon the sense of duty of every officer and non-commissioned officer, and the personal pride and gentility of every enlisted man, to effectually preclude looting and other abuses committed for personal advantage. He feels certain that officers and men who have so important a duty to perform, and who are forced to adopt such radical measures to accomplish it, do not wish to reflect serious discredit upon their motives by seeking or desiring any personal advantage.

J.F. BELL.

NO. 23.   DECEMBER 28th, 1901.

TO ALL STATION COMMANDERS:

Hereafter no one in the territory of this Brigade will be permitted to use or have in their possession war bolos or talibons, that pattern of bolo which is long and sharp-pointed like a sword, except municipal police, constabulary, native scouts and others duly authorized to carry them.

In the provinces of Batangas, Laguna and Tayabas all such bolos found in possession of others than those mentioned above will be seized by troops and will be turned in to the commanding officers of scout companies, constabulary or municipal police until all such organizations are fully supplied with an equipment of bolos, which they should be required to carry on all occasions in case they have no bayonets.

In the province of Cavite peaceful citizens who have in their possession war bolos or talibons, left over from the war period, may be permitted to retain them, provided they accompany troops or soldiers detailed for the purpose to a blacksmith to have them cut off so as to leave the blade square and blunt at the outer end and not exceeding fourteen inches in length. All war bolos of those who do not wish to have them so modified will be taken up and turned in to the government. Unoffending citizens who are friendly to the United States in those portions of Tayabas which may be considered peaceful will be accorded the same privilege as that accorded above to the peaceful citizens of Cavite.

No one will interfere with the right of municipal police, native scouts, interpreters or soldiers to carry war bolos when properly authorized to do so.

J.F. BELL.

NO. 24.   DECEMBER 28th, 1901.

TO ALL STATION COMMANDERS:

All municipal police, *cabezas* and local officials of garrisoned towns in this Brigade should be warned that they will be held responsible for neglect of duty if they knowingly permit Malvar, Caballes, Gonzales, Casala, Dimaculangang, Marques or any other insurgent leaders or soldiers to enter or take refuge in their towns or barrios (if occupied by people) without arresting them or immediately reporting their presence to the military authorities. In the provinces of Batangas and Laguna persons offending against the provisions of this order will be immediately brought to trial by Military Commission or Provost Court, depending upon office held and the degree of culpability in the offense committed.

In case local officials or police report the presence of insurgents who are found gone on the arrival of troops, commanding officers will make a searching investigation with a view to ascertaining whether they have not been warned before their presence was reported and will take steps to effectually preclude the possibility of a repetition of such duplicity. In any case that can be clearly proven the officials or police guilty of the duplicity will be brought to trial by Military Commission.

J.F. BELL.

NO. 25.   JANUARY 2nd, 1902.

TO ALL STATION COMMANDERS:

If there are any persons from the provinces of Batangas and Laguna who should be arrested for complicity in the insurrection and who have left and gone to Manila, they can be arrested and returned as prisoners of war if their names are telegraphed to these Headquarters. When telegraphing information, all that is known about the person's whereabouts in Manila, where his relatives live, etc., and in what way he has been complicated in the insurrection will be stated.

J.F. BELL.

NO. 26.

TO ALL STATION COMMANDERS:

In view of the possibility that negotiations for a general surrender in this Brigade may follow operations now being conducted, it is desired to compile at these Headquarters as accurate statistics as possible relating to all persons who are now serving as officers in connection with the insurrection and relating to the total number of guns which are supposed to be under command of Malvar at the present time, in order that a complete surrender of all guns and officers under his control, as commander-in-chief, may be exacted.

With this in view, all station commanders will immediately telegraph to these Headquarters the names of all officers now out who pertain to their towns, and the number of guns in possession or under control of such leaders. Where a number of guns have been turned over to towns by insurgent leaders in the past this number should also be stated and the number, if any, that have been captured out of said lot.

Owing to delay in communication, it is important that this information be furnished promptly on receipt of this message.

J.F. BELL.

NO. 27.

JANUARY 3rd, 1902.

TO ALL STATION COMMANDERS:

Any unexpended balance of Provost Court fines, which may be in the possession of station commanders in this Brigade, will be used to purchase rice or palay at once before it becomes scarce and high-priced, which rice and palay will be stored and carefully kept for issue to paupers and people who are absolutely without means, under the provisions of General Orders No. 64, Headquarters Division of the Philippines, series 1900. Officers will attend to this matter at once.

Acknowledge receipt and report action.

J.F. BELL.

NO. 28.   JANUARY 9th, 1902.

TO ALL STATION COMMANDERS:

Information reaching these Headquarters indicates that the hardship and pressure which has been brought upon the people by the campaign has caused them, in seeking revenge or means of self defense, to resort to their well known expedient of false denunciation. Inasmuch as this custom is a pernicious nuisance and might become a serious impediment to the success of military operations, commanding officers in the provinces of Batangas and Laguna will promptly bring to trial by Provost Court, for conduct prejudicial to good order and military operations, any person who makes a false denunciation, whenever it can be established to the satisfaction of the commanding officer that said false denunciation has been knowingly and viciously made for purposes of revenge, of self defense, of clouding the real issue, of throwing discredit upon the transactions, motives or testimony of material witnesses, or for any other purpose.

Inasmuch, however, as it is not intended to prevent or discourage the making of legitimate complaints, commanding officers will take great pains to investigate carefully and bring no one to trial until it has been clearly ascertained that they have made false denunciations knowingly and purposely with vicious intent.

Any kind of defiance of the government or disloyal manifestation against measures adopted by it, to put an end to the insurrection in this Brigade, will be suppressed at once. The people must be taught the necessity for submission to the legally constituted authority and this can be properly done in one way only—by firm and relentless repressive action.

J.F. BELL.

NO. 29.   JANUARY 9th, 1902.

TO ALL STATION COMMANDERS:

I am leaving Batangas tomorrow for the field, to be gone probably for some weeks. It is desired that officers study their instructions carefully and try to settle all questions to the best of their own judgement without applying here for further instructions, except where it may be absolutely essential.

In case I must be communicated with, address telegrams to Adjutant General, Batangas, who will be kept informed of my whereabouts.

J.F. BELL.

NO. 30.   JANUARY 23rd, 1902.

TO ALL STATION COMMANDERS:

In order to keep the enemy constantly on the move, wear them out, and deprive them of food, detachments will continually be sent out from all towns, scouting for the enemy, and hunting for food supplies cached by insurgents. Whenever these supplies cannot possibly be saved, and when a guard cannot be left until transportation can be sent for, they will be destroyed, but the Brigade Commander again desires to call the special attention of all officers to the urgent necessity of saving all food supplies and increasing the same as much as possible by planting, in order to preclude the coming of hunger and want.

The Brigade Commander hopes that all officers, especially station commanders, will understand and realize that care in preventing hunger and want among the people who have voluntarily assembled within zones of protection, has become, under conditions existing now, quite as important an obligation on their part as the conduct of military operations. Fully as much credit will attach to successful efforts in this regard as to the faithful performance of other military duties.

To this end the following measures may be adopted wherever the people have assembled within protected zones:

1st.   It will be made known to the people, men, women and children, that they may accompany scouting parties for the purpose of securing food and will be permitted to retain all they can transport or carry. In case no one desires to go, some able bodied men with pack ponies will be impressed and compelled to accompany detachments.

Any available transportation at the post which can be spared and used, without conflict with the interests of the service, may be used in bringing in caches of food supplies, which will be retained and stored for future issue. None of this food will be used for government purposes.

2nd.   All standing crops will be harvested under such protection and supervision as can be given by patrols.

3rd.   Should it become necessary or desirable, in the provinces of Batangas and Laguna, all available food supplies may be taken possession of by the government and be equitably and economically distributed for the benefit of all alike.

4th.   As many of the inhabitants as possible will be assigned plots of ground on which to cultivate new crops, within protected zones, preferably by equitable arrangement with the owners thereof, but irrespective of ownership if necessary in the provinces of Batangas and Laguna, and no matter whether the people want to work or not they will be required to plant pieces of land assigned them. Land owned by absentees may be assigned for cultivation without reference to them.

5th.   All owners will be permitted and encouraged to plant food crops on land not situated so far within the mountains as to render it impossible to give laborers any protection whatever. Such laborers will be required to leave within protected zones all their stores of food supplies, taking with them to their work only such small quantities at a time as may be necessary for their daily subsistence.

6th.   The attention of all officers is invited to the contents of Sections 7, 14, 21, 37, 38, 155 and 156, G.O. 100. Inasmuch as it can be safely assumed that at one time or another since this war began, every native in the provinces of Batangas and Laguna (and in the provinces of Cavite and Tayabas also) has, with exceedingly rare exceptions, taken some part in aiding and assisting the insurrection against the United States, they have all rendered themselves liable to being compelled to bear their share of the burden and hardship of a war for which they are directly responsible. Therefore, whenever it may become necessary to prevent hunger, want or starvation, in the provinces of Batangas and Laguna, war contributions may be levied upon all persons of means to provide for the necessities of those who have been brought to a condition of want by the results of a war really promoted and brought about by the wealthy and influential classes. But it is not intended that this method of feeding the poor shall be adopted except as a last resort, and before adopting any such method, local commanding officers will communicate with these Headquarters, explaining the necessity therefore and the plan it is proposed to follow.

J.F. BELL.

NO. 31.   JANUARY 26th, 1902.

TO ALL STATION COMMANDERS:

Arrangements have been made with the Chief Commissary of the Division to supply second grade rice of good quality on calls from commissaries for sale to the inhabitants of all towns where the food supply may become exhausted in the provinces of Batangas and Laguna, and where, on account of closed ports, no food can be otherwise imported. The Chief Commissary has made a contract for a large number of pounds of this rice at $1.58 gold per hundred pounds, or about four pesos and a half per cavan. It will be obtained and distributed through the Subsistence Department under the provisions of the following regulations:

1st. All local and regimental commissaries will make requisition for the quantity which can undoubtedly be disposed of (and no more) upon the distributing commissaries from whom they have been in the habit of securing their subsistence supplies. These requisitions will be made by telegraph, on receipt of this circular, stating about when the rice should be delivered. Towns which are sub-posts to others or have no local commissaries should obtain their supply of rice from the commissary of their main town.

These commissaries who have been drawing their rations direct from Manila are authorized to communicate direct with the Chief Commissary of the Division, with reference to rice so needed.

2nd. All distributing commissaries in Batangas and Laguna will consolidate the estimates received and telegraph the amounts to the Chief Commissary of the Division direct. In case any one of the posts which local, regimental or distributing commissaries supply (either on ration return or by invoice) fails to make an estimate as directed above, they will telegraph to the commanding officer or commissary at that post for the purpose of ascertaining whether any rice will be needed, before forwarding their estimates.

3rd. The commissaries at Batangas, Calamba and Santa Cruz will act as distributing commissaries, in this connection, for all towns to which they now ship subsistence supplies.

4th. On arrival of the rice by water at towns or distributing points, it will be transferred by government land transportation, when sufficient is available, to the point from which it was called for, free of cost. Whenever there is not sufficient land transportation for this purpose, commanding officers are authorized to impress and pay a reasonable price for such transportation as may be available at the town in order to bring from the point of landing the rice ordered for sale to the people, but no addition will be made to the selling price on account of the use of this or government transportation.

5th. Rice thus transferred will be invoiced to local commissaries, or wherever there are no local commissaries, the commanding officer must collect from the town sufficient money to pay cash for rice ordered when it leaves the subsistence storehouse at the distributing point. Where it is not practicable to do this, and commanding officers are willing to have the rice charged to them personally, local, regimental and distributing commissaries are authorized to make credit sales to said commanding officers, to be paid for when sold by them, it being understood that all accounts must be fully settled at the end of each month, as is usual in credit sales.

In every such town rich people or dealers can usually be found who will agree to take from commanding officers, at the invoice price or more any surplus rice remaining unsold and thus no risk of loss need be run by commanding officers, who, after there is no further need of sales direct to the people, will be authorized to dispose of any balance to the wealthy or dealers.

In no case will any of this rice be sold to natives on credit, and officers actually making sales to natives will be held accountable that the government is paid the invoice price of every pound sold by them.

6th. Until further orders, none of this rice will be sold without special authority to dealers or anyone else in large quantities at one time. It is expressly desired and intended that, as long as present conditions last, the rice shall be sold in small quantities at a time and under the direct supervision of army officers and their military agents, under such restrictions as will effectually prevent any of it coming into the possession of insurgents.

7th. To the laboring class and poor people this rice will be sold at a small advance over cost price, but to all other persons a profit will be charged of about 25 per cent., as a rule, charging more or less only where circumstances justify or necessitate it.

8th. A strict and accurate account will be kept of all such rice sales, showing profit made after paying the Subsistence Department the invoice price therefor, and this profit will be retained in the hands of commanding officers as a reserve fund for the purpose of purchasing rice for gratuitous issue to paupers, who are unable by reason of age or infirmity to work, or for issue to people absolutely without means, in return for labor, in case such issue should become necessary.

9th. In no case will any gratuitous issue of rice be made to those who are able to work without exacting a corresponding amount of labor on roads, bridges or other public utilities, as a daily rate of compensation not exceeding a day's ration of rice for those who labor and for such actual members of their families as are too old or too young or too infirm to be able to labor.

All able bodied members of the family, both male and female, will be expected to work for food which may be issued the family free of cost.

10th. A strict enforcement of the foregoing provisions is of the utmost importance. No one can foresee how long it may be necessary to care for the population and prevent hunger, and officers are cautioned not to make, under any circumstances, gratuitous issues of rice to persons who are able to buy or work for the same. The common people of these Islands easily become pauperized and would, without hesitation or scruple, accept subsistence and remain idle as long as the government would continue to feed them. Officers should exercise the utmost economy of their resources and not become liberal and generous simply because they have accumulated a considerable fund and because it seems no longer necessary to practice rigid economy. Any funds which may be left on hand may be badly needed to purchase seed for poor people or assist them in other ways in recovering from the effects of the war. It is intended that all this money shall be finally expended for the benefit of the people, and they should be made to understand that the government is not pretending to give them an amount of food which is equivalent to a day's wages, but that it means to require them to work for a living only, until such time as the insurrection ends and they may be able to resume their normal pursuits in safety, without military protection.

11th. The attention of all officers is invited to the fact that they may collect three pesos from all those who are able to pay, and prefer not to work on roads, which money is available to pay wages to those who do work, said wages not in any case to exceed a peseta per day, and it is hoped that this provision, in connection with those announced in Circular Telegram No. 30, will enable the people to buy food and be sufficient to preclude the necessity of involving the government in any expense whatever.

12th. For adult paupers, and children too young to work, no more that two chupas of rice per day for the former and one for the latter will be issued gratis at present. Children over twelve years of age should work, and for each man, woman and child who works not exceeding two and one half chupas of rice for adult and two chupas for children will be issued.

13th. The palay and rice heretofore gathered and stored for future disposition by the government will be disposed of under the provisions of this order, two measures of palay being issued in lieu of one of rice.

14. Officers are again cautioned not to begin gratuitous issues of rice or issues in lieu of labor until want makes it absolutely necessary and to take every precaution to prevent abuses and impositions.

To this end, accurate registers of families will be prepared with the assistance of local native officials, and great care will be taken to see that children or other persons are not registered as belonging to more than one family and that children are not borrowed in order to swell the size of issues due.

15th. Captain George H. Morgan, 3rd Cavalry, Acting Chief Commissary of the Brigade, is hereby placed in general supervision of the enforcement of the provisions of this circular and those contained in No. 30, and the commanding officers of Santa Cruz, Calamba, Batangas and Balayan, will each designate an officer to assist him in the supervision of districts which will later be defined by him.

J.F. BELL.

NO. 32. JANUARY 26th, 1902.

TO ALL STATION COMMANDERS:

To insure success in the important consideration of preventing hunger and want, the Brigade Commander has, in the provisions of Circulars 30 and 31, authorized methods which may possibly create in the minds of some an impression that greater leniency in enforcing the policy heretofore adopted is desired.

To prevent any misapprehension in this regard, the Brigade Commander desires it understood that he considers a firm adherence to the stringent measures outlined by previous circulars (and amplified but not modified by these two) is absolutely essential to our success in this Brigade.

He therefore enjoins upon all commanding officers that they permit no relaxation in the strict enforcement of orders, unless especially authorized from these Headquarters, and such authority will be given, as a rule, only in those towns which have become completely loyal and have secured the surrender to the government of all the guns contained in their jurisdiction.

J.F. BELL.

NO. 33. FEBRUARY 12th, 1902.

TO ALL STATION COMMANDERS:

The attention of all officers in this Brigade is invited to the provisions of G.O. 100, which preclude the killing of any person who can be captured and a strict compliance with the spirit of that order is hereby enjoined upon all.

J.F. BELL.

NO. 34. FEBRUARY 12th, 1902.

TO ALL STATION COMMANDERS:

The attention of officers is invited to the desirability of promptly paying for all guns surrendered or turned in by any person, as said payment is sure to encourage renewed efforts on the part of natives to secure the surrender or turning in of guns. Orders direct the payment for serviceable guns only, but, in interpreting this order, guns which would not be considered sufficiently serviceable to arm American troops can nevertheless be paid for as, in the hands of natives, they are all sufficient to accomplish their purpose in terrorizing and imposing upon the population at large.

It is our purpose to obtain all guns, irrespective of class or caliber, as any gun in the hands of ladrones is a source of terror to the people of barrios and sparsely settled outlying districts. Shot guns and obsolete weapons may therefore be paid for and revolvers may also be purchased at twenty pesos each.

J.F. BELL.

NO. 35. FEBRUARY 15th, 1902.

TO ALL STATION COMMANDERS:

The provisions of Circular Telegrams, authorizing officers to impress transportation whenever necessary for field service, was not intended to preclude payment of a reasonable compensation.

It is desirable that said transportation be paid for in order to enable the people to buy food. It is also intended that those who are required to labor on roads be paid three pesos each for their 15 days labor from the funds collected for that purpose from those who pay in preference to working. Engineer officers supervising work in this Brigade will pay for labor at the same rates as prescribed herein, and will take steps to see that an accurate account is kept and that each person who labors 15 days gets credit and pay therefor.

J.F. BELL.

NO. 36.

TO ALL STATION COMMANDERS:

In accepting surrenders, all commanding officers will have tabular lists prepared showing names of persons, grades, corps or companies, residence, including barrio and pueblo, class of guns, chief of column or company, whether surrendered or captured, with place and date, and also remarks.

Those surrendering will be required to surrender documents, and the list referred to above will include the names of all collectors, agents and civil officials associated with those surrendering. The lists will likewise include the names of all persons who have ever belonged to or been associated with such bodies of troops, indicating what disposition has been made of them, and if captured, dead or surrendered, showing when and where. This information should all be obtained from those surrendering.

After the surrender is concluded, copies of these lists will be forwarded direct to to the Provost Marshal of the Brigade.

J.F. BELL.

NO. 37.

April 7th, 1902.

TO ALL STATION COMMANDERS:

Owing to the changed condition of affairs throughout the Brigade, it is no longer considered necessary or desirable to enforce the restrictions heretofore placed upon the quantity of rice which might be sold to any person at one time.

It has been observed that these restrictions have made it difficult for the people to obtain rice, necessitating their losing much time waiting their turn to purchase daily supplies, thus depriving them of opportunity to use this time in earning money with which to buy.

It is desirable that every commanding officer now address himself to the problem of distributing the rice in such manner as to involve the least practicable loss of time to the people in securing it.

With this end in view, all restrictions will be removed as to quantity to be sold at one time, inasmuch as it will make little difference at present whether some of it gets into the hands of insurgents or not. Precaution should be taken, however, to prevent the purchase of rice in quantities exceeding the family necessities of the purchaser, for speculative purposes.

With a view of facilitating a prompt and satisfactory distribution thereof, it may be transferred at a wholesale price to certain authorized and reliable persons, who will agree to give bond not to sell it at more than a fixed rate. Such persons should be required to sell at all hours of the day at a price not exceeding 25 cents Mex. per ganta when sold at retail, or $6.00 Mex. per cavan when sold by cavan or larger quantities. To such persons the commissary is authorized to sell the rice at not exceeding $5.50 Mex. per cavan, but the privilege of thus retailing it will be accorded to Filipinos only, and not to persons of other nationalities.

It should be understood by all venders that any violation of the conditions of their privilege, especially charging more than the fixed price for rice, or giving short measure, will forfeit the amount of the bond, which should in no case be less than $200.00 Mex., and where large quantities are sold, not less than $300.00 Mex.

The number of venders should be fixed so that purchasers can be accomodated without undue loss of time, and they should be so distributed as to be most convenient to the entire pueblo.

A close inspection should be maintained on the weights and measures of venders and in order that they may have no excuse for overcharging, rice should be sold to them by weight, 140 pounds (including weight of the sack) being considered a cavan. One cavan is supposed to be placed in each sack shipped by the Subsistence Department in Manila but on arrival at stations it is generally found to have wasted some pounds. All wastage and losses should fall on the profit which is gained in its sale, and not be permitted to fall on the government.

It is possible that in some small pueblos as soon as the restriction as to quantity purchasable at one time is removed, it may not be necessary to adopt the method herein outlined, as it may be found that the government can distribute direct with sufficient facility and promptness, but wherever necessary to accomodate the people promptly, two or more distributing stations where the rice can be secured, should be established under charge of reliable soldiers or non-commissioned officers.

J.F. BELL.

NO. 38.

May 16th, 1902.

TO ALL STATION COMMANDERS:

In view of the fact that all insurgents have now surrendered in Batangas and Laguna, it is desired to put a complete end to every war measure heretofore authorized and enforced and to re-establish a feeling of security and tranquility among the people as rapidly as possible. With this end in view:

1st. All secret service agents will be discharged and all investigations will be stopped, excepting such as relate to the crime of assassination. These will be continued only in cases where American prisoners have been assassinated, or where aggrieved relatives appeal for justice.

2nd. The amount of secret service funds now on hand will be reported to these Headquarters by wire and will be sent as soon as possible and invoiced to 1st Lieutenant Daniel Van Voorhis, 3rd Cavalry, Aide de Camp to the Brigade Commander.

3rd. All restrictions upon occupations and privileges usually pursued and enjoyed in times of peace, which were imposed by Telegraphic Circulars, will cease to be enforced as directed in instructions heretofore given. With the exception of exercising such supervision as may be necessary to an honest collection and expenditure of municipal revenues, to the prevention of unauthorized practices, to the enforcement of quarantine and sanitary regulations, and to rectifying injustice, it is desired that commanding officers leave the internal government of towns as much as possible to the people or to the officers who have been appointed or elected for that purpose.

4th. All authority heretofore given to impress laborers and means of transportation is hereby revoked. It is desired that no steps be taken which will interfere with the cultivation of fields by the people, and that every encouragement and assistance be given to the planting and raising of a new crop.

5th. Commanding officers will make an effort to ascertain the owners of all animals now in the possession of troops which have been captured or taken up in the country, and upon proof of ownership, will return them to their proper owners. This will be accomplished with as little delay as possible.

6th. It is desired that as much assistance shall be given to poor natives as may be practicable in the reconstruction of their houses and in other industries. Steps will be taken, where needed, to procure palay, camotes and corn for planting, and also necessary hand tools for agriculture. Wherever poor funds are available, commanding officers are authorized to spend a portion thereof for this purpose.

7th. It is not intended in this circular to revoke the provisions of Telegraphic Circulars heretofore published for the purpose of regulating the procuring and distributing of rice to natives wherever such government assistance may be needed.

J.F. BELL.

TELEGRAPHIC MEMORANDUM.

BATANGAS, P.I., January 16th, 1902.

To ALL STATION COMMANDERS,
  BATANGAS AND LAGUNA:

Following memorandum repeated for your information and guidance:

"DIRECTIONS FOR VACCINATION OF NATIVES.

Surgeons will supervise vaccination within protected zones and sub-posts tributary to their hospital.

Native vaccinators should work in parties of two, accompanied by a detailed soldier. The party should be supplied with 100 units of virus, probe with small bulb end, scalpel, alcohol and cotton for cleansing, and blank book on which date, street (or barrio), and names of all vaccinated should be entered.

Radiating from crowded centers, the party should enter first the most crowded houses, and move inmates to the farthest room. Then working at doorway, natives are led out singly, and each (of any age) not showing pock marks, vaccinated.

The four functions of recording, cleansing (by rubbing a small area with a bit of cotton moistened with alcohol), scraping and applying virus with probe, should be equally divided between the two vaccinators.

As many, children especially, will evade vaccination, the protected zones must be repeatedly gone over till no unscratched arms remain.

Bauan has vaccinated 5,000 natives with 2,500 units of virus. When half of the supply of virus is exhausted, the number vaccinated, number of working days, and amount of virus left will be reported to this office, and an estimate will be forwarded showing how much more is required.

Surgeons should occasionally accompany working parties to insure thoroughness and effective rapidity, varying from foregoing details when necessary.

Vaccinators proving unsatisfactory should be immediately replaced, reporting new names to this office.

Soldiers, padres and influential natives can assist greatly in developing a favorable public opinion, which should immediately realize that this compulsory measure is for the good of each and every individual in the territory concerned.

(Signed).   WM. STEPHENSON,
                   Major , Surgeon, U.S. Army,
                             Chief Surgeon."

The prompt vaccination of all persons living within protected zones is of the utmost importance, and post commanders will give their personal attention to this matter.

Wherever opposition is met by vaccinators, commanding officers will detail sufficient troops to round the people up and compel them to submit to vaccination.

Whenever the number of vaccinators authorized is insufficient, the number hired may be increased.

To the posts of Batangas, Calamba and Santa Cruz, virus will be sent for distribution to all posts tributary thereto. At these posts virus must be kept on ice until it is sent to the posts to which addressed. It will be transmitted as promptly as possible. All other posts in the district will be furnished virus direct.

Information concerning payment of vaccinators will be transmitted to post surgeons by the chief Surgeon of the Brigade.

It can easily be understood by all how serious the difficulty and detriment to our plan of campaign would be, should an epidemic of small-pox break out in any protected zone. Therefore the importance of prompt completion of this compulsory vaccination should be impressed upon all concerned.

Copies of this telegram will follow by mail. Vaccine is en-route and must be kept as cool as possible. Acknowledge receipt.

J.F. BELL.

GENERAL ORDERS.

------0-----

FEBRUARY 27th, 1902.

GENERAL ORDERS,
    No. 8. }

The following orders governing pack animals carrying ammunition will be strictly carried out.

Hereafter, when troops are traveling or scouting in this Brigade, pack animals carrying ammunition must be closely watched, or led by an individual detailed for the especial purpose, who will be held accountable for any loss of said ammunition by the straying of the pack animal.

It is enjoined upon all commanders of troops that they use the utmost endeavor to have the greatest vigilance exercised in this regard.

By Command of Brigadier General Bell:

MILTON F. DAVIS,
Captain, 1st Cavalry,
A.G.

March 25th, 1902.

General Orders,
No. 12. }

Pursuant to telegraphic instructions from Headquarters of the Army, dated March 2, 1902, and promulgated in letter from the Adjutant General, Division of the Philippines, March 4, 1902, the maintenance of Military prisons, and the support of military prisoners, including members, or former members, of the military establishment, camp followers, prisoners of war and persons convicted by Court Martial, Military Commissions or Provost Courts of specific offenses against the laws of war, is a charge against the appropriation for the support of the army.

The support of persons, including insurrectos, convicted by Civil Courts, Military Commissions, Provost Courts, or other tribunals, of common law crimes, or for violation of the penal code, or the revenue laws, or of offenses against public order in the Philippine Islands, is a proper charge against Insular appropriations, notwithstanding the charge be laid as a violation of the laws of war.

Though natives not in the military service of the United States may be convicted by Military Commissions and Provost Courts of crimes mentioned in the 58th Article of War, the crimes being charged as offenses against the "laws" of war, (such persons not being subject to trial for violations of "Articles" of War), the maintenance of such prisoners (notwithstanding their convictions of "offenses against the laws of war") is properly chargeable against Insular appropriations, inasmuch as all the offenses specified by the said article are common law crimes.

Of natives not belonging to the military service, who are convicted by Military Courts, it is intended to charge to appropriations for the support of the army the maintenance of only those who have been convicted of political offenses (which are not common law crimes), in violation of the laws of war, and when convicted of both political offenses and common law crimes the maintenance of the individual will be charged to Insular appropriations.

Commanding officers, officers in charge of prisoners, and commissary officers, are cautioned to use careful discrimination in complying with G.O. No. 90, Division of the Philippines, 1900, and G.O. No 70, Division of the Philippines, 1901.

The principal application of this order will be in submitting separate ration returns for the two classes, which will be done invariably.

In order that military appropriations may be reimbursed for rations issued to prisoners which are chargeable to the Insular treasury, issuing commissaries will forward each month, through military channels, certified copies of all ration returns on which rations have been issued to prisoners, whose maintenance is chargeable to Insular appropriations, together with a consolidated return of such ration returns.

By Command of Brigadier General Bell:

MILTON F. DAVIS,
Captain, 1st Cavalry,
A.G.

March 27th, 1902.

General Orders, }
    No. 13. }

Intelligence officers will send to these Headquarters reports on slips of all important persons of the towns in which they are stationed, whom they know to have been implicated in any way with the insurrection. This should include active sympathizers, aiders, abettors, contributors, collectors, civil insurgents officials and insurgents who have been soldiers or officers, and information should contain all that is known of the individual stated in detail.

Similar reports should also be made upon all local municipal officials and parish priests, stating whether loyal, disloyal or suspected of disloyalty, giving reasons on which opinions are based.

Other reports should likewise be made on all individuals who have rendered any especially valuable service to the Government, stating in detail the character of the services rendered.

A card eight inches long and three and a quarter inches wide (similar to the card partially illustrated below), will be used in making such reports.

By Command of Brigadier General Bell:

MILTON F. DAVIS,
Captain, 1st Cavalry,
A.G.

Name

Age   Race $\left\{\begin{array}{l}\text{Married.}\\ \text{Single.}\end{array}\right.$

Residence (Pueblo and Barrio)

Occupation

Relations with insurrectos

(Here follows a brief political history of the individual, giving the information called for in the order.)

GENERAL ORDERS, }
    No. 2. }

I.   To avoid the uncertainty and confusion that must otherwise inevitably arise, all station commanders who have, or may have, native prisoners under their charge, will cause the following information in regard to each prisoner to be prepared and kept as a part of the permanent records of that station.

Name, age, race (Tagalog or otherwise), residence, occupation, date and place of arrest or capture, by whom confined, charges or reason for arrest fully stated; whether tried, and if so, by what tribunal, with sentence awarded and date of same, date of release or transfer and by whose order.

Prisoners transferred from one station to another will be accompanied by descriptive list applicable to their cases.

II.   At the end of each calendar month station commanders will forward to the Brigade Provost Marshal at these Headquarters a "Report of Native Prisoners". This report will be a transcript from the records of prisoners at that station.

Prisoners held for investigation for less than a month and released before end of month because nothing is developed against them or those likewise held as witnesses and released before end of month need not be included in this report.

III.   Charges against natives triable by Provost Courts may be referred by station commanders to the most convenient Provost Court for investigation and trial. Such charges will be accompanied by a list of witnesses and all other information obtainable that may facilitate the trial of the case.

In this connection the attention of station commanders is invited to the last Par. of General Orders No. 356, c.s. Division of the Philippines.

IV.   Each Provost Court will keep an accurate record in book form of all cases tried by him in which shall be entered the name of the accused with occupation and place of residence, charges and specifications, list of material witnesses, findings and sentence with date and signature of court.

In addition, a brief summary of the testimony in important cases and any other information that may be useful for the consideration of the Brigade Commander, will be noted.

V.   At the end of each calendar month, Provost Courts will submit to the Brigade Provost Marshal a "Report of Cases Tried" together with the original charges on which will also be endorsed, the plea, findings and sentence. The report of cases is for transmittal to Department Headquarters. The original charges will be filed at these Headquarters.

By Command of Brigadier General Bell:

MILTON F. DAVIS,
Captain, 1st Cavalry,
A.G.

PROCLAMATIONS AND CIRCULAR LETTERS.

------o------

PROCLAMATION.

May 16th, 1902.

To the People of Batangas,
        Laguna and Mindoro:

The war is concluded. This proclamation is published to announce the desire of the Brigade Commander that peace conditions may be re-established in these provinces as speedily as possible. For this purpose he has directed all of his subordinates to remove all restrictions which have been placed upon trade, traffic and travel, and upon fishing and other occupations and privileges enjoyed by the people during peace.

All captured animals now in possession of the government will be returned to owners who can prove ownership. All other private property, excepting such houses as may be necessary for the accommodation of the United States forces, will also be returned. The government intends to pay a reasonable rent for all houses from the first of May, and to pay back rent to all persons who can prove that they did not contribute or take part in the insurrection against the United States.

All military authorities in these provinces desire to assist the people as much as possible and to settle all just claims.

The Brigade Commander hopes that the people can look upon officers and soldiers as their friends, and they are reminded that if they desire the friendship of others, they must show themselves friendly to them.

> J.F. BELL,
> Brigadier General, U.S. Army,
> Commanding.

CIRCULAR LETTER.

May 16th, 1902.

To all Commanding Officers,
        Provinces of Batangas, Laguna and Mindoro:

As is well known, the vigorous and relentless enforcement of severe measures has been repeatedly insisted upon from these Headquarters in order to accomplish results which, it was believed, could be accomplished in no other way. The end in view has now been attained.

Confidently relying upon the well established generosity of American officers and men toward conquered enemies, the Brigade Commander desires to appeal to all officers and men to use their utmost influence in bringing about a complete and radical change in the policy heretofore enforced in order that the people may become convinced that the military power in these Islands is not only able but willing to befriend them to a degree quite as great as its ability to conquer them when necessary. In order to accomplish this result the Brigade Commander begs of all officers and men co-operation and assistance as generous and spontaneous as has been accorded him during the past five months.

In view of the amount of punishment which has been inflicted (by hardship and suffering) upon the foolish and stubborn members of the community, it is not believed that any generous officer or soldier can fail to feel sorry for them, especially for the poor and ignorant. It is therefore earnestly requested that officers and men not only make a special effort to treat natives with consideration and justice, but that they also endeavor to display a kindly feeling whenever brought in contact with them.

An opinion is very commonly entertained that the animosities and resentments engendered by war unfit officers and men of the army to establish and supervise local governments satisfactory to the people of these Islands. I cannot concur in this opinion, and it is my hope that by the time civil government is re-established in these provinces the feeling of the people toward the military branch of the service will demonstrate the incorrectness of this theory.

It seems apparent that one difficulty in gaining the confidence of the more ignorant class of natives has been our inability to get into close personal contact with them or to obtain accurate knowledge of their troubles and grievances. The *presidente*, who is the usual source of communication with the common people, is not always reliable in this regard. It is therefore suggested to commanding officers, if they can find in their commands intelligent non-commissioned officers and enlisted men, able to communicate with natives, who take an interest in their welfare, that they assign certain outlying barrios to the especial case of such non-commissioned officers and men, and encourage them to spend as much of their time therein as may be consistent with the performance of their regular guard duties. They should be permitted to visit these barrios and live therein as much as possible with a view to becoming thoroughly acquainted with the people and gaining their confidence in order that they may have someone whom they can rely on to represent their needs or grievances to the commanding officer. Of course it is not meant to suggest that the people be told the object of this plan, or that grievances or complaints be solicited, neither will it be of any service to encourage or prefer requests or grievances which it is impracticable to grant or abate, but the reason no relief can be extended should be explained. When poor people have some legitimate request or complaint to make and are accompanied to the commanding officer by an American soldier to present it for them, they will come to believe that officers and soldiers take a real interest in their welfare.

Whenever there are sufficient subordinate officers at a post, the jurisdiction should be divided between them, each being assigned a portion to especially look after and to supervise the efforts of the non-commissioned officers and soldiers assigned thereto.

It is desired that no arbitrary or unnecessary exactions be indulged in or permitted with the people, and that, so far as practicable, the same relations be established and adhered to in dealing with them as now exist in pacified provinces. It is also desired that the service of secret agents be dispensed with and that crimination and re-crimination be discouraged and listened to as little as is consistent with the interest of the government in these provinces. It is not considered best to foment, stir up or investigate, for the present, past political delinquencies of natives, nor is it considered desirable to act on suspicion any longer. Before any action is taken looking to the arrest of anyone, who may be denounced in the future for intriguing against the government, it would be well be examine carefully into the motive of the accuser, with a view to ascertaining whether he is not seeking to satisfy a private grievance or thirst for revenge. Some indiscreet talk on the part of foolishly proud but ignorant men, smarting under the humiliation of defeat, is to be expected, but in view of the present impotency of the irreconcilable element, it is believed that the interest of the government and of peace and tranquility will be better subserved by ignoring such harmless ebulitions of bad temper than by seeking to punish hasty and excited expressions, which, though possibly treasonable, are without real influence.

This letter will be read to all officers and men of this command.

Respectfully,

J.F. BELL,
Brigadier General, U.S. Army,
Commanding.

MEMORANDUM FOR COMMANDING OFFICERS.

(To Accompany Circular Letter of May 16th, 1902.)

MAY 16th, 1902.

Such commanding officers as detail non-commissioned officers or soldiers to care for barrios, under provisions of accompanying circular letter, should caution them that they are not expected to take charge of the barrio or in any way to become officious; that they are not sent there in the capacity of detectives to get people into trouble or to interfere with the peace and tranquility of the barrio; that they should try to become well acquainted with and gain the confidence of the *cabezas,* and that should they find them pursuing practices which they know to be prohibited by law they should ask to eradicate such illegal practices by counselling and advising *cabezas* rather than by seeking to have them punished. Where the abuses are serious, however, and the *cabezas* are not amenable to advice, and where the people feel aggrieved the *cabezas* should be reported to the commanding officer for discipline. They should be cautioned that they are not expected to hunt up grievances nor expected to accomplish anything suddenly, and that they should not be so vigorous or so zealous in seeking evidence touching complaints and grievances as to arouse hatred, antagonism or resentment between residents of the barrio. Wherever practicable, disputants should be pursuaded to settle their differences and grievances amicably.

They are simply expected to gain the confidence of the people and befriend them when necessary, but shall seek to accomplish their results with tact, patience and perseverance, with a view to promoting the welfare, tranquility and harmony of the barrio rather than to stirring up strife or recrimination. They should never act on the statements of one side alone, where a dispute between the people is involved, but if complaints are of any consequence or merit, should take their time ascertaining the truth by consulting the other side and consulting them in such a tactful way as not to stir up animosity on their part against their accusers. Unless the service is tactfully performed more harm is liable to result than good. The most important thing is to exercise patience and perseverance and not to form judgements hastily. There is no need of haste and they should take plenty of time to learn the real truth. The ascertaining of the truth under such circumstances is generally difficult and requires time.

It is desired that they help and befriend the people as much as possible in any way that seems practicable. If some of the people are miserably poor and have no seed to plant, these facts should be reported to the commanding officer, and by him to these headquarters in case he has no means of supplying their needs.

NOTE.—When this circular letter and memorandum were issued it was understood that civil government would not be re-established for a matter of six months or more in Batangas, Laguna and Mindoro.

CIRCULAR LETTER.

JULY 4th, 1902.

To THE HONORABLE CIVIL
   GOVERNOR OF THE PROVINCE OF _____

Sir:—

In view of the recent establishment of Civil Government in your province, I desire to express to you and to your associate officials my cordial sympathy with the purposes of the Philippine Commission in your nomination and in the establishment of Civil Government in this Brigade, and to assure you and your associates that I desire to co-operate in every proper way in promoting peace and contentment among the people, and the material prosperity of your province. My cordial co-operation in this line will always be at your service.

Until civil provincial government is fully established in all respects, the military forces must necessarily continue to perform certain functions which it is their desire and duty to turn over to the civil administration whenever it is prepared to assume such obligations.

During this interval of divided responsibilities, it can scarcely be expected that mistakes can be entirely avoided by inexperienced officers and non-commissioned officers who have had no previous experience in making discriminations between civil and military obligations and prerogatives in such a case of divided responsibility.

Should such mistakes on the part of the military officials occur anywhere within your province, it will only be necessary to represent them to the Brigade Commander to have them promptly rectified.

Local presidents should understand that all wrongs or abuses committed by military persons should be promptly reported to the local commanding officer, and that in case this action does not result in a satisfactory rectification of grievances, they should refer the matter to you for presentation to the Brigade Commander.

I inclose for your information a copy of instructions for the guidance of troops which have this day been transmitted to all local commandants of towns in this Brigade.

Assuring you of my highest regard and consideration for you and your associates, believe me,

Very sincerely and respectfully,

J.F. BELL,
Brigadier General, U.S. Army,
Commanding.

CIRCULAR LETTER.

JULY 4th, 1902.

To all Officers,
    Third Separate Brigade:

In view of the fact that civil government has been established in this Brigade, I desire to invite your especial attention to the following extracts from instructions contained in General Orders No. 179, Headquarters Division of the Philippines, series 1901:

"I.   That where municipal police are organized, and, except as prescribed in Par. 2, of this order, all United States troops * * * * abstain from any and all attempts at coercion, control, influence or interference with the administration of civil affairs.

The troops will at once be put under an efficient state of discipline and instruction, to the end that no disorder may be charged to their account or annoyance caused the civil administration by reason of their presence. The conduct of the troops should facilitate rather than retard the maintenance of order, and all military persons will, by their example, show proper respect for civil administration and for all civil officers.

*   *   *   *   *   *

II.   As a rule, interference by the military in civil affairs will correspond to the well known procedure in the United States.

When, under an emergency, the civil governor of the Philippine Islands shall make a request upon the Commanding General of the Division of the Philippines for the assistance of troops, the latter will be governed by such instructions as they may receive from these headquarters.

*   *   *   *   *   *

In this connection the attention of all officers is invited to the general regulations governing such duty as outlined in Articles LII, paragraphs 436–491, inclusive, Army Regulations of '95, and article LIII, paragraphs 563 to 568, inclusive, Regulations of 1901.

In cases where the assistance of the military arm has been asked for, full report of the fact with attending circumstances, action taken and result thereof, will be promptly submitted through regular military channels."

*   *   *   *   *   *

All officers should now realize that the relations which have heretofore existed between them and the local civil officials have become radically changed. This relation is no longer that of superior and subordinate, but purely a business relation, such as that which should exist between an officer and any other person (independent of his authority) with whom he is brought into business relations by an exigency of the service.

Should the rights or interest of officers or their commands be deleteriously affected by indifference on the part of local civil functionaries to their official obligations, or injuries result from their failure to enforce local ordinances and regulations, officers will confine their actions to dispassionate representation of the facts in writing to local presidents, requesting action in abatement of the nuisances or injuries complained of, but it is not intended by these instructions to authorize or encourage harassing complaints to local officials simply because their conduct of affairs does not come up to what the local commander may consider a proper standard, especially *not* in matters which do not directly and materially concern the welfare and interest of the commanding officer and his command.

Should this course not result in rectification of grievances, an explanation to that effect, accompanied by a copy of communications to and from the local president and by a statement of any other pertinent circumstances, will be forwarded to the Brigade Commander, who will lay the matter before the civil governor of the province in case he deems it necessary or desirable.

It is especially desired that all officers conduct themselves with forbearance, consideration, discretion and tact, and require a strict compliance from members of their commands with all local regulations and legitimate orders.

When any official or inhabitant complains of abuses or wrongs committed by military persons, the local commander will investigate the matter and in case complaint be found worthy, do what he can to see that reparation is made or satisfaction is given by the offender, or punish him by court martial, and, in case he has not sufficient authority to make complete reparation, he will report the matter to the Brigade Commander for further instructions.

It is desired that all military persons seek to maintain friendly relations with local civil officials and accommodate them when it can be appropriately done without detriment to the interests of the public service.

Copy of letter this day sent to the civil governor of the province is enclosed for your information.

Very respectfully,

J.F. BELL,
Brigadier General, U.S. Army,
Commanding.

PROCLAMATION.

JULY 22nd, 1902.

TO THE PEOPLE OF THE
    PROVINCE OF BATANGAS:

1st. Hereafter, whenever government wagons or pack mules are passing along the highways loaded with rice for sale to the people, any person living more than one mile from the poblacion of any pueblo may offer six pesos to the wagon or pack master and obtain therefor a sack of rice.

The rice cannot be thus sold in less quantities, but several families can unite in buying a sack. It is strictly prohibited, however, that they pay more than six pesos per sack in any case.

2nd. In order to assist poor people as much as possible wagon masters and teamsters have orders to permit people found traveling in the road on foot to ride in government wagons as far as they wish to follow the road, whenever the said wagons are traveling empty or have light loads.

In furnishing this accommodation, preference will always be given to women and children. Persons carrying bundles or packages may take these burdens with them on the wagons. They will be permitted to dismount from the wagons wherever they may wish to do so.

J.F. BELL,
Brigadier General, U.S. Army,
Commanding.

100

CIRCULAR LETTER.

COMMANDING OFFICERS,
  BATANGAS PROVINCE:

In order to accommodate and assist the poor people as much as possible in the distribution of rice, by wagon or pack train, commanding officers, commissaries and quartermasters will hereafter see that the necessary orders are given to wagon and pack masters to insure a safe and systematic carrying out of the following provisions:

1st.   On the payment of six pesos to the wagon or pack master by any native who lives more than one mile from the poblacion of any pueblo the wagon or pack master will deliver to that person one sack of rice, and on arrival at his destination will turn in to the commanding officer or commissary the six pesos in lieu of every sack of rice thus sold. Under no circumstances will more than six pesos be charged or accepted.

2nd.   Whenever government wagons are traveling on highways empty, wagon masters or teamsters will permit the people walking along the road to ride, preference being always given to women and children when there are more people than the wagon will hold.

Even when wagons are not empty, but loads are light, people will be permitted to ride provided roads are not so bad as to inflict an undue burden upon the animals. Teamsters will halt to take on and put off the people wherever they may be found desirous of riding or may wish to get off. The Brigade Commander hopes that teamsters and wagon masters will take an interest in extending this courtesy and accomodation to those whom they find walking in the road.

A proclamation in Spanish and Tagalog announcing to the people that they may avail themselves of the privileges mentioned in this order has been distributed throughout the Province of Batangas.

BY COMMAND OF BRIGADIER GENERAL BELL:

MILTON F. DAVIS,
Captain, 1st Cavalry,
A.G.

APPENDIX.

-------o-----

TELEGRAMS OF THANKS AND CONGRATULATIONS.

DECEMBER 10th, 1901.

MAJOR PITCHER,
      MINDORO:

Referring to your acknowledgement of receipt of Telegraphic Circulars 1, 2 and 3, it has been my intention to inform you that these circulars would be sent to you for your information, guidance and authority in so far as they are applicable in your judgement to the situation in Mindoro. It is my intention to leave the management of affairs on that Island entirely within your discretion, but to furnish you the same authority, assistance and support accorded to everyone else. Congratulations upon your good work.

J.F. BELL,
Brigadier General, U.S. Army,
Commanding.

JANUARY 6th, 1902.

CHIEF SIGNAL OFFICER,
      NORTH PHILIPPINES, MANILA:

I have now sent the last Telegraphic Circular I contemplate sending at present, a fact which affords me quite as much satisfaction and relief, as I know it will afford the personnel of your corps serving in connection with this Brigade. Mail facilities are so very slow and uncertain here that had it not been for the exceptionally valuable service rendered me by your corps in connection with my work I feel morally certain I could not have accomplished in six months results which have already been accomplished in six weeks. I wish to extend to you, and through you to every man and officer in your corps, who has participated in this labor, my sincerest thanks for the service rendered me and his government in this connection. I have not failed to realize that they have been called upon and taxed in quite an unusual manner, but I think they will also realize that they have been assisting in a very hard campaign, worked out under very unusual conditions. The rapidity of such success as we have attained depends almost exclusively upon the very exceptional and valuable service the members of your corps have rendered me, at least such rapidity could not have been achieved without their assistance. Please thank each individual for me.

J.F. BELL,
Brigadier General, U.S. Army,
Commanding.

"HEADQUARTERS DEPARMENT OF NORTH PHILIPPINES.

MANILA, April 16th, 1902.

BRIGADIER GENERAL J.F. BELL, LIPA:

The Department Commander, Major General Loyd Wheaton U.S.A., thanks you and the officers and men of the Third Brigade for the results of the operations ending with the surrender of Malvar. The methods pursued and the ability, energy and efficiency displayed by you and your command will be a model for future operations against the resistance of semicivilized people to the arms of the United States. By Command of Major General Wheaton.

WALTZ, A.A.G."

"HEADQUARTERS DEPARMENT OF NORTH PHILIPPINES.

MANILA, April 19th, 1902.

GENERAL BELL, BATANGAS:

Following telegram repeated for your information: Headquarters Division of the Philippines, Manila, April 19th, 1902. Gen. Wheaton, Manila, P.I.: The following cablegram is repeated for your information and transmission to General Bell: Washington, D.C., April 17, 1902. Chaffee, Manila: Acting Secretary of War directs me to inform you that the President wishes through you to express his gratification and the gratification of the American people at the results of the campaign of J.F. Bell and officers and men of his command in Batangas and Laguna Provinces, which culminated in the surrender of insurgent forces under Malvar and which will further extend the territory in which civil government is exercised.

CORBIN."

"The pleasure which I feel because of the President's congratulations for General Bell, his officers and men is difficult for me to express in words. No body of American troops has ever before been charged with a duty more difficult of accomplishment, except (with reference to terrain only) our comrades in the Island of Samar. So unique has been the situation in many ways that no one not an actual participant can appreciate the conditions met with to be overcome, nor fully determine the necessary means to accomplish the object in view, namely, compel recognition of United States authority, that peace and order might prevail in the disturbed section. General Bell and his troops will desire that you, General, share with them, as Department Commander, the congratulations of the President because of your never failing encouragement and watchfulness over their labors. (Signed), CHAFFEE." "By Command of MAJOR GENERAL WHEATON.

WALTZ, A.A.G."

HEADQUARTERS THIRD SEPARATE BRIGADE, DEPARMENT OF NORTH PHILIPPINES.

MAY, 16th, 1902.

TO THE OFFICERS AND MEN,
      THIRD SEPARATE BRIGADE:

With profound satisfaction the Brigade Commander announces that so far as is known at these Headquarters, every insurgent officer and band heretofore operating in the Provinces of Batangas and Laguna has been captured, killed or forced to surrender, and it is believed, from the evidence of residents of these two provinces, that conditions therein have never heretofore been more peaceful than they are at the present time.

This condition has been brought about by a campaign lasting less than four months, and such signal success as has been achieved therein is attributed by the Brigade Commander to the zealous, loyal and uncomplaining support which has been given by every officer and man in this Brigade to plans and instructions which were formulated for the conduct of the campaign.

The Brigade Commander, being fully aware of the difficulties which have been encountered and overcome, of the tireless energy and persistence displayed by all and the fatigue and sickness which has resulted therefrom, only needs to add that his thanks and appreciation, gratefully extended to each individual officer and man, are in due proportion to the heavy burden of responsibility which has been lifted from his shoulders through the success achieved by their untiring efforts and loyal zeal.

By Command of Brigadier General Bell:

MILTON F. DAVIS,
Captain, 1st Cavalry,
A.G.

HEADQUARTERS THIRD BRIGADE, DEPARTMENT OF LUZON.

Batangas, P.I., October 10th, 1902.

To the Presidente of

———————————————————

Sir:—

You doubtless know that a certain sum of money has been accumulated by the sale of rice in this province. It is desired to spend this money for the benefit of the inhabitants of the province, and for this purpose we have purchased and brought to Batangas some modern agricultural implements very generally used in the United States.

Through the kindness of the Secretary of the Interior and of the Chief of the Bureau of Agriculture in Manila, we have been furnished with other implements, and have all ready begun some experimental work on a piece of land near this town with the ultimate purpose of establishing a permanent experimental station somewhere in the province.

Having already received orders to return to the United States and expecting to leave the Islands within a short time, I would like to consult the municipal officials of the pueblos, as well as other persons who are interested in the welfare of the people and the advancement of agriculture, concerning the best manner of employing this money for the benefit of the province.

I therefore hope that you will attend the assembly of *presidentes* in this pueblo, which will take place on the 20th instant. Will you please invite all the other officials and *consejales* of your pueblo who might wish to come with you.

I would also like you to notify all persons of your pueblo, largely interested in agriculture, that the modern implements, of which I have spoken above will be exhibited in Batangas on the 20th, and possibly the 21st, instant, and all those who would like to see them will be cordially welcomed. If it be possible, practical trials will be made of all the implements in order to illustrate to the spectators the manner of using each machine.

We have also a variety of American seeds for gardens, fields and *haciendas* which will be distributed for experimental purposes to those who may desire them.

Very respectfully,

J.F. BELL,
Brigadier General, U.S. Army,
Commanding.

NOTE:—It was intended to include this circular letter with the others pertaining to reconstruction, but its absence escaped observation until after the rest had been set up and printed.—M.F.D.

MEMORANDA BY GENERAL BELL.

-----0-----

NOTE: —The following Memoranda are the result of experience with operations and administration in this Brigade. Thcy were prepared by General Bell, for his own future information, as actual occurrences brought the matters mentioned to his attention from time to time. With his permission they are included in this pamphlet under the belief that the data contained therein might become equally useful to others.—M.F.D.

It has become evident that the purpose which inspired the publication of Telegraphic Circular No. 18 was not explained therein with sufficient accuracy, clearess or detail. Some commanding officers, apparently possessing a correct impression of the purpose of the order, have been able to promptly produce desired results by the arrest and confinement of some of the most prominent offenders only. The less prominent ones then completely changed their political attitude and tendered their services for the re-establishment of peace for their pueblos.

By thus arresting one or two or a few of the most prominent offenders at a time, every day or so, and by giving no explanation of the cause of arrest to anyone, less prominent offenders (deprived of the counsel and support of these dominant leaders of character and determination) become nervous and apprehensive, lose courage, and render assistance for fear their turn may come next. Additional information is thereby gained concerning the complicity of the more prominent persons who, in the meantime, should be held as prisoners and be permitted to communicate with no one, but should be informed of what has been learned concerning their acts. In a very short time these leaders (who exercise the dominant influnce) realizing the futility of further resistance and concealment, will volunteer to render all the assistance in their power, in order to escape punishment for their past political offenses. It will not take them long to become convinced that the military authorities have secured sufficient evidence to convict them, and this will insure their fidelity to promises.

In this manner, through personal interest, or self protection, the entire community can be converted from partisans of insurrection into partisans of peace.

On the contrary, some commanding officers, misconstruing the spirit and the purpose of the circular (which unfortunately was expressed in a rather ambiguous way) arrested on the same day every representative of the classes mention therein, with few or no exceptions, and without sufficient effort to make wise and useful discriminations. Misery loves company, and when all the prominent persons of a community find themselves thus incarcerated, they derive strength, consolation, satisfaction and support from companionship and from realization that they are all in the same boat. Confined together, they can mutually encourage and sustain each other and being in close contact, they all become subject to the personal domination of the stronger minded and more determined partisans of insurrection. They are thus liable to maintain their nerve and determination to continue resistance.

This wholesale arrest and lack of discrimination also creates resentment and may convert into enemies the few who may be indifferent or wavering or secretly desirous of peace. It may unite the entire community in one common resolve. For the above reasons it may become much more difficult to bring about a break in their ranks or determination and to get them started upon voluntary efforts for peace.

Whenever circumstances are such as to render wholesale arrests essential (as is sometimes necessary in cases of wide spread conspiracy or desperate intimidation) efforts should be made to place the more prominent offenders in solitary confinement where they cannot communicate with anyone or use their influence to dominate the ordinary crowd of followers. In fact this method is a very efficacious plan in any case of determined resistance where sample facilities are at hand for thoroughly carrying it out.

It is of great importance that unceasing efforts be made to ascertain as soon as possible who the real dominant leaders of the town are. Also whether there is a very general conspiracy to which all are equally committed, or if there be possible partisans of peace. Whether all are united by universal sympathy or the majority under the influence of desperate intimidation from the few.

Circular 18 should have been revised and explanation of its purpose have been made in greater detail.

It is necessary to reach the common people through the influence of the dominant classes. Therefore nothing should be done to unnecessarily humiliate or arouse the resentment of the latter. For this reason it is a mistake and bad policy to require *principales* to work in policing their prisons and streets as was done in some instances until prohibited.

In order to break up the insurgents' organization, completely destroy their influence and convert the people from partisans of war to partisans of peace, in towns where the people are characterized by such intelligence as enables them to exercise good judgement and common sense, it has been found very useful (after they have very generally lost hope of their power to continue successful resistance, and have really begun to work for peace) to offer all prominent persons of dominant influence an opportunity to make a full and complete confession of their connection with the insurrection, under a promise of immunity from punishment for anything they confess. The reason of this is as follows: Many persons, deeply complicated themselves, are prevented from making bold and earnest efforts to assist in the re-establishment of peace by fear that such a change of policy on their part might bring down upon them denunciation from persons whose resentment is liable to be aroused by their change of attitude. They are consequently reluctant to take the chance of arousing resentment through dread of personal consequences. After they have made a clean breast of every thing and been pardoned, however, they realize that there is absolutely nothing that they can be denounced for and have thereby acquired a suitable status for beginning a radical change of conduct.

Deprived of the further assistance and influence of these persons, after this plan has been successfully applied, insurgents become utterly unable to re-organize their department of supply, security and information in these towns.

In order to preclude partial confessions, those to whom the opportunity is offered should be informed that if anything is afterwards discovered, which they have failed to confess, they will be subject to trial and punishment for that particular conduct.

There are some small towns where all the people are too ignorant to appreciate such a proposition, and can only be influenced by punishment. It is therefore necessary to exercise discrimination in adopting this expedient.

Notwithstanding all the prominent male persons of a very irreconcilable pueblo, who were deeply complicated in the insurrection, had been arrested and confined for a considerable time, they remained resolute and the entire pueblo persisted in denial of all knowledge of insurgents or their whereabouts, insisting that they had not seen or heard of an insurgent for months. The commanding officer finally discovered that the female relatives of the insurgent leaders of the town were secretly carrying on a system of supply and information and were keeping up communication between those confined in the pueblo and those in command of troops in the mountains. All insurgents were regularly supplied by these relatives, who, being women, had no difficulty in sending supplies and warning of all that Americans did to husbands, brothers and other relatives belonging to the insurgent column of the town.

On discovering this, the commanding officer secured a large dwelling house in the pueblo and built a high stockade fence around the yard. Having made his preparations and secured a list of the wives, sisters and other close female relatives of insurgent officers and leaders in the pueblo, they were arrested and detained in the quarters prepared for them. They were well fed and cared but a sentinel was placed at the gate of the stockade and another patrolled around it, absolutely prohibiting any communication whatever with them.

Insurgents in the field, thus cut off from communication with their families, became very uneasy, and, unable to longer secure food or maintain a satisfactory understanding with the pueblo, finally surrendered in a body to secure the release of their families and friends and to obtain food.

A similar enlightening incident occurred in another pueblo where the ranking insurgent officer, a colonel, had left his family. The commanding officer treated them with consideration and kindness and soon became very friendly with them. He was in the habit of chaffing the wife about her insurgent husband and she finally offered to try to induce him to surrender. She did not succeed and tearfully informed the commanding officer that he really wanted to surrender, but having taken an oath to continue in the field as long as the others did, he was ashamed to abandon them.

The commanding officer jokingly remarked that he guessed the best way to get her husband was to arrest her, whereupon she appeared to consider this a bright idea and replied that it might not be a bad plan after all.

Securing a suitable house for her accommodation, he arrested and detained her there under guard. Early the next morning the husband presented himself in full uniform, and, handing his sword to the commanding officer, begged that he release his wife and confine him in her place. He was accomodated and held in confinement until he had agreed to use his influence and work for peace by inducing his command to surrender.

This expedient of the commanding officer had simply presented to his mind an obligation which he considered greater than that he owed his comrades. He did want to surrender but lacked an excuse to satisfy his Quixotic price. The supposed misfortunes of his wife, suffering on his account, offered a satisfactory one.

The immortal Don Quixote originated a word to express an old idea and conferred upon a nation the reputation of being the most Quixotic in the world. The Spaniard is doubtless very Quixotic but his one time ward, the educated Filipino, has been a very apt pupil and has gone away beyond his teacher in his acquirement of this quality, though possibly in modified form. This circumstance should never be forgotten in dealing with him.

Judging from experience in this war, a much greater length of time is always required to settle claims and outstanding obligations of the government, after a campaign is concluded, than is required to successfully conclude the campaign itself. After the close of the war in the Ilocano region it required six months of the hardest and most disagreeable kind of labor to properly dispose of prisoners and to settle all outstanding claims and obligations of the government. This delay and unnecessary trouble resulted from the careless way in which officers (burdened by the responsibilities and labor of a very active campaign) had universally neglected to make proper reports of evidence against prisoners and of operations in seizing or taking possession of property for use of the government.

Unending subsequent trouble would be saved if, at the beginning of every war and campaign, especial efforts were made to impress upon officers the importance of the following precautionary measures:

In taking possession of buildings or other property for public use, the officer ordering the same should put his order in writing and give one copy thereof to the owner, if he can be found. The order should plainly show the owner's name, kind of property, date on which taken possession of and for what purpose. The property should be described, and, when ascertainable, its value, together with daily or monthly rental value, be stated approximately. If it be a house it should be stated whether it was occupied (and in what manner) when taken possession of or was vacant.

The political attitude of owner should be stated when positively known. When not *positively* known it should be stated "unknown". If the owner is absent in insurrection, that fact should also be stated.

In case of a house appropriated with the owner present, he should be required to take possession of and remove all movable property not needed for temporary use. Memorandum receipt should be given for all movable property retained for the temporary use of troops.

For the protection of the officer, it is advisable that he take from the owner an acknowledgment that he is in possession of all his personal and movable property except that for which he holds receipt. The inventory of property retained for use of the government should be made in the presence of witnesses who should attest it. One copy of inventory, certified by witnesses, should be delivered to the owner and one copy retained by those in possession of the property. Reports should be made to Brigade or District Headquarters at once of all seizures, giving full history of case and accompanied by copies of the order of seizure, inventories, etc. It is important that this memoranda, concerning property taken possession of, be carefully preserved.

Whenever cattle are taken to furnish food to troops, a receipt should be given to the owner, if practicable, which should show approximate size and value of animals. All food supplies seized for soldiers and grain and other forage seized for animals, should be likewise receipted for, showing amount in each case and approximate value in community. Owners of all means of transportation seized for use of troops should be given receipts showing kind and character of transportation, time used and approximate value, together with daily or monthly rental value in locality. If staff officers are present with funds, private property seized for use or consumption should always be paid for at once.

An officer seizing food supplies and forage for use of his command, far in excess of the regulation allowance of same, as shown by ration and forage returns, will remain personally responsible for the excess.

Money should never be seized unless there is positive proof that it belongs to the hostile government and unless there is a respectable amount of it. It is unnecessary and useless to seize very small sums, and they give more trouble than they are worth. No one should ever be permitted to seize jewelry under any circumstances, unless it be *perfectly* clear that large amounts of public funds have been converted into expensive and valuable jewelry in order to preserve said funds from seizure or to facilitate transportation.

All money or jewelry necessarily seized should be carefully counted and inventoried in the presence of those from whom seized and other witnesses, all of whom should sign as witnesses to correctness of inventories.

The seizure of valuable jewelry for the purpose of influencing the owners to surrender is always liable to lead to scandal, and should never be permitted.

Officers who are desirous of avoiding complications or the necessity of disagreeable subsequent investigations, will always be careful to take no arbitrary action which cannot be justified as a military necessity by the laws of war, and, whenever it may become necessary to seize private property for public use, to take possession of it in a systematic and prescribed way. They will remember that claims will certainly be afterwards made by owners of the property. They will be especially cautious that in case of seizure of money, it be turned in with a report to the next superior headquarters as soon as practicable. It is never permissible or safe to make any unauthorized use thereof, for it can be assumed as a certainty that claims will eventually be made for all money and property seized, and any carelessness or lack of system in taking possession or delay in making reports of action in such matters cannot fail to cast reflection upon the officer who is responsible therefor.

In destroying property, by way of retaliation or as a military necessity, an inventory should always be made and authenticated by witnesses, when practicable, showing quantity and assigning approximate values to everything destroyed. A full and complete report should be made at once to next higher headquarters of the action taken and the reasons for taking it.

No large quantities of food should ever be destroyed except when there is real danger of its falling into the hands of the enemy and when it is absolutely impracticable to move and place it under the care of a permanent detachment at the nearest station. If practicable, a guard should be left with it until transportation can be sent for or until its location, kind and quantity can be reported to the District or Brigade Commander, who may wish to make other arrangements to guard or send for it.

The foregoing precautions have attained an increased importance because of the more liberal provisions for the protection of strictly private property adopted by all civilized nations as a result of the Peace Conference of 1899 at the Hague. (See G.O. 52, A.G.O., series 1902.)

In hostilities conducted by civilized nations, in accordance with the provisions of the laws of war, it is not customary to expect or depend upon material aid from non-combatants not regularly employed by the belligerent forces. The important subjects of Security, Information and Supply, of civilized belligerents, are attended to by forces regularly designated or departments especially organized and conducted for that purpose by officers and enlisted men in uniform and by such civilian employees as may be hired to assist therein. Except in the case of spies and other secret agents, their occupation and employment is not secret but well known. The service usually done by war traitors is so well performed by these hired spies, and by the department organized for that purpose, that there is little need of a pacific citizen becoming a spy or war traitor in aid of his government.

As a consequence, it is not a matter of very great importance, in regular warfare, when operating against a civilized nation, whose belligerent forces are well organized, to especially hunt for, detect and punish spies and war traitors among the non-combatant and apparently pacific inhabitants of the country.

In guerrilla warfare, however, (in the Philippines Islands, as well as elsewhere,) it is seldom that an insurgent force has a regularly organized department or method of performing the service of Security, Information and Supply. It must, perforce, depend upon the voluntary or forced assistance of the inhabitants of its own country for security, information and supplies, and for transmitting correspondence and verbal intelligence between the component fractions of the insurgent forces.

In the Philippine Islands, it has been very frequently, if not generally, the case that a considerable percentage of the apparently pacific population has secretly served insurgents in the capacity of spies, collectors, agents, cargadores, etc., for the collection and distribution of information and supplies. Though a part of this service is expected (and exacted by intimidation) of all inhabitants in common, some persons are usually secretly selected and designed as collectors, spies and special agents, to make collections and see that those who refuse to contribute, or who aid the enemy, are assassinated.

It has also been customary for insurgents to regularly and secretly organize all able-bodied, non-combatant, apparently pacific males, of towns, barrios and sitios, into militia or reserves. These organizations, in addition to other duties, habitually maintain innocent looking outposts, unarmed and dressed in ordinary clothing, whose duty it is to secretly transmit to armed insurgents timely warning of the presence of any hostile force or danger.

In the insurrection against the United States Government in the Philippine Islands, it has been very common for municipal officials, (including *presidentes* and other town officials, *consejales* and *cabezas* or *tenientes* of barrios) who are serving under authority of the American Government, to secretly perform exactly the same duty on behalf of the insurgent force. Cases have been known where officials have collected just double the tax prescribed by law, in order that they might make an impartial division of the revenue between Americans and Insurgents.

To bring a campaign to a successful close within a reasonable length of time, or to put a prompt end to insurrection, under such conditions, it is of the *first importance* to adopt and enforce measures for detecting and punishing all persons, who, (posing as peaceful citizens) secretly aid, assist, protect, collect supplies or give comfort to the enemy in any way, with a view to breaking up the insurgent organization for procuring information and supplies.

Such persons should be imprisoned and, when competent evidence is obtainable, be brought to trial by provost courts and military commissions. In awarding punishment it is advisable that they be given both imprisonment and fine.

It frequently happens that, in order to avoid punishment for complicity, they volunteer and render valuable assistance in bringing the insurrection to a close. Whenever desirable to reward such service with leniency, it is advisable, instead of granting them a full pardon, simply to suspend their punishment during good behavior.

It has sometimes occured that men sentenced to pay fines, have, as soon as pardoned, made claims against the government for damages which might have been offset by the fines had they not been revoked by pardon. By suspending sentences, the fines can always be used as offsets against such claims, and will discourage the making of false and unjust claims.

At the end of campaigns, when peace has been re-established, it is a so customary to pardon and release all prisoners, convicted of political offenses only. For reasons cited in the above paragraph, it is likewise advisable to release and, by military order, suspend their sentences instead of revoking them by pardon.

Section II

General Orders 100*

Laws of War: General Orders #100, 1863. "Instructions for the Government of Armies of the United States in the Field." 24 April 1863. Appears on website www.yale.edu/lawweb/avalon/lieber.htm. Specific articles emphasized by Brigadier General J. Franklin Bell in his 1901–02 *Telegraphic Circulars* to his subordinates in southwestern Luzon are highlighted in **BOLD** print.

General Orders 100 [Lieber Code]

GENERAL ORDERS No. 100.

WAR DEPT., *ADJT. GENERAL'S OFFICE,*

Washington, April 24, 1863.

The following "Instructions for the Government of Armies of the United States in the Field," prepared by Francis Lieber, LL.D., and revised by a board of officers, of which Maj. Gen. E.A. Hitchcock is president, having been approved by the President of the United States, he commands that they be published for the information of all concerned.

By order of the Secretary of War:
E.D. TOWNSEND,
Assistant Adjutant-General.

INSTRUCTIONS FOR THE GOVERNMENT OF ARMIES OF THE UNITED STATES IN THE FIELD.

SECTION I.—*Martial law—Military jurisdiction—Military necessity—Retaliation.*

1.   A place, district, or country occupied by an enemy stands, in consequence of the occupation, under the martial law of the invading or occupying army, whether any proclamation declaring martial law, or any public warning to the inhabitants, has been issued or not. Martial law is the immediate and direct effect and consequence of occupation or conquest.

The presence of a hostile army proclaims its martial law.

2.   Martial law does not cease during the hostile occupation, except by special proclamation, ordered by the commander-in-chief, or by special mention in the treaty of peace concluding the war, when the occupation of a place or territory continues beyond the conclusion of peace as one of the conditions of the same.

3.   Martial law in a hostile country consists in the suspension by the occupying military authority of the criminal and civil law, and of the domestic administration and government in the occupied place or territory, and in the substitution of military rule and force for the same, as well as in the dictation of general laws, as far as military necessity requires this suspension, substitution, or dictation.

The commander of the forces may proclaim that the administration of all civil and penal law shall continue either wholly or in part, as in times of peace, unless otherwise ordered by the military authority.

4.   Martial law is simply military authority exercised in accordance with the laws and usages of war. Military oppression is not martial law; it is the abuse of the power which that law confers. As martial law is executed by military force, it is incumbent upon those who administer it to be strictly guided by the principles of justice, honor, and humanity—virtues adorning a soldier even more than other men, for the very reason that he possesses the power of his arms against the unarmed.

5. Martial law should be less stringent in places and countries fully occupied and fairly conquered. Much greater severity may be exercised in places or regions where actual hostilities exist or are expected and must be prepared for. Its most complete sway is allowed—even in the commander's own country—when face to face with the enemy, because of the absolute necessities of the case, and of the paramount duty to defend the country against invasion.

To save the country is paramount to all other considerations.

6.   All civil and penal law shall continue to take its usual course in the enemy's places and territories under martial law, unless interrupted or stopped by order of the occupying military power; but all the functions of the hostile government—legislative, executive, or administrative— whether of a general, provincial, or local character, cease under martial law, or continue only with the sanction, or, if deemed necessary, the participation of the occupier or invader.

7.   Martial law extends to property, and to persons, whether they are subjects of the enemy or aliens to that government.

8.   Consuls, among American and European nations, are not diplomatic agents. Nevertheless, their offices and persons will be subjected to martial law in cases of urgent necessity only; their property and business are not exempted. Any delinquency they commit against the established military rule may be punished as in the case of any other inhabitant, and such punishment furnishes no reasonable ground for international complaint.

9.   The functions of ambassadors, ministers, or other diplomatic agents, accredited by neutral powers to the hostile government, cease, so far as regards the displaced government; but the conquering or occupying power usually recognizes them as temporarily accredited to itself.

10.   Martial law affects chiefly the police and collection of public revenue and taxes, whether imposed by the expelled government or by the

invader, and refers mainly to the support and efficiency of the Army, its safety, and the safety of its operations.

11. The law of war does not only disclaim all cruelty and bad faith concerning engagements concluded with the enemy during the war, but also the breaking of stipulations solemnly contracted by the belligerents in time of peace, and avowedly intended to remain in force in case of war between the contracting powers.

It disclaims all extortions and other transactions for individual gain; all acts of private revenge, or connivance at such acts.

Offenses to the contrary shall be severely punished, and especially so if committed by officers.

12. Whenever feasible, martial law is carried out in cases of individual offenders by military courts; but sentences of death shall be executed only with the approval of the chief executive, provided the urgency of the case does not require a speedier execution, and then only with the approval of the chief commander.

13. Military jurisdiction is of two kinds: First, that which is conferred and defined by statute; second, that which is derived from the common law of war. Military offenses under the statute law must be tried in the manner therein directed; but military offenses which do not come within the statute must be tried and punished under the common law of war. The character of the courts which exercise these jurisdictions depends upon the local laws of each particular country.

In the armies of the United States the first is exercised by courts-martial; while cases which do not come within the Rules and Articles of War, or the jurisdiction conferred by statute on courts-martial, are tried by military commissions.

14. Military necessity, as understood by modern civilized nations, consists in the necessity of those measures which are indispensable for securing the ends of the war, and which are lawful according to the modern law and usages of war.

15. Military necessity admits of all direct destruction of life or limb of armed enemies, and of other persons whose destruction is incidentally unavoidable in the armed contests of the war; it allows of the capturing of every armed enemy, and every enemy of importance to the hostile government, or of peculiar danger to the captor; it allows of all destruction of property, and obstruction of the ways and channels of traffic, travel, or communication, and of all withholding of sustenance or means of life from the enemy; of the appropriation of whatever an enemy's country

affords necessary for the subsistence and safety of the Army, and of such deception as does not involve the breaking of good faith either positively pledged, regarding agreements entered into during the war, or supposed by the modern law of war to exist. Men who take up arms against one another in public war do not cease on this account to be moral beings, responsible to one another and to God.

16. Military necessity does not admit of cruelty—that is, the infliction of suffering for the sake of suffering or for revenge, nor of maiming or wounding except in fight, nor of torture to extort confessions. It does not admit of the use of poison in any way, nor of the wanton devastation of a district. It admits of deception, but disclaims acts of perfidy; and, in general, military necessity does not include any act of hostility which makes the return to peace unnecessarily difficult.

17. War is not carried on by arms alone. It is lawful to starve the hostile belligerent, armed or unarmed, so that it leads to the speedier subjection of the enemy.

18. When a commander of a besieged place expels the non-combatants, in order to lessen the number of those who consume his stock of provisions, it is lawful, though an extreme measure, to drive them back, so as to hasten on the surrender.

19. Commanders, whenever admissible, inform the enemy of their intention to bombard a place, so that the non-combatants, and especially the women and children, may be removed before the bombardment commences. But it is no infraction of the common law of war to omit thus to inform the enemy. Surprise may be a necessity.

20. Public war is a state of armed hostility between sovereign nations or governments. It is a law and requisite of civilized existence that men live in political, continuous societies, forming organized units, called states or nations, whose constituents bear, enjoy, and suffer, advance and retrograde together, in peace and in war.

21. The citizen or native of a hostile country is thus an enemy, as one of the constituents of the hostile state or nation, and as such is subjected to the hardships of the war.

22. Nevertheless, as civilization has advanced during the last centuries, so has likewise steadily advanced, especially in war on land, the distinction between the private individual belonging to a hostile country and the hostile country itself, with its men in arms. The principle has been more and more acknowledged that the unarmed citizen is to be spared in person, property, and honor as much as the exigencies of war will admit.

23.   Private citizens are no longer murdered, enslaved, or carried off to distant parts, and the inoffensive individual is as little disturbed in his private relations as the commander of the hostile troops can afford to grant in the overruling demands of a vigorous war.

24.   The almost universal rule in remote times was, and continues to be with barbarous armies, that the private individual of the hostile country is destined to suffer every privation of liberty and protection and every disruption of family ties. Protection was, and still is with uncivilized people, the exception.

25.   In modern regular wars of the Europeans and their descendants in other portions of the globe, protection of the inoffensive citizen of the hostile country is the rule; privation and disturbance of private relations are the exceptions.

26.   Commanding generals may cause the magistrates and civil officers of the hostile country to take the oath of temporary allegiance or an oath of fidelity to their own victorious government or rulers, and they may expel every one who declines to do so. But whether they do so or not, the people and their civil officers owe strict obedience to them as long as they hold sway over the district or country, at the peril of their lives.

27.   The law of war can no more wholly dispense with retaliation than can the law of nations, of which it is a branch. Yet civilized nations acknowledge retaliation as the sternest feature of war. A reckless enemy often leaves to his opponent no other means of securing himself against the repetition of barbarous outrage.

28.   Retaliation will therefore never be resorted to as a measure of mere revenge, but only as a means of protective retribution, and moreover cautiously and unavoidably—that is to say, retaliation shall only be resorted to after careful inquiry into the real occurrence and the character of the misdeeds that may demand retribution.

Unjust or inconsiderate retaliation removes the belligerents farther and farther from the mitigating rules of regular war, and by rapid steps leads them nearer to the internecine wars of savages.

29.   Modern times are distinguished from earlier ages by the existence at one and the same time of many nations and great governments related to one another in close intercourse.

Peace is their normal condition; war is the exception. The ultimate object of all modern war is a renewed state of peace.

The more vigorously wars are pursued the better it is for humanity. Sharp wars are brief.

30.   Ever since the formation and coexistence of modern nations, and ever since wars have become great national wars, war has come to be acknowledged not to be its own end, but the means to obtain great ends of state, or to consist in defense against wrong; and no conventional restriction of the modes adopted to injure the enemy is any longer admitted; but the law of war imposes many limitations and restrictions on principles of justice, faith, and honor.

SECTION II.—*Public and private property of the enemy—Protection of persons, and especially of women; of religion, the arts and sciences— Punishment of crimes against the inhabitants of hostile countries.*

31.   A victorious army appropriates all public money, seizes all public movable property until further direction by its government, and sequesters for its own benefit or of that of its government all the revenues of real property belonging to the hostile government or nation. The title to such real property remains in abeyance during military occupation, and until the conquest is made complete.

32.   A victorious army, by the martial power inherent in the same, may suspend, change, or abolish, as far as the martial power extends, the relations which arise from the services due, according to the existing laws of the invaded country, from one citizen, subject, or native of the same to another.

The commander of the army must leave it to the ultimate treaty of peace to settle the permanency of this change.

33.   It is no longer considered lawful—on the contrary, it is held to be a serious breach of the law of war—to force the subjects of the enemy into the service of the victorious government, except the latter should proclaim, after a fair and complete conquest of the hostile country or district, that it is resolved to keep the country, district, or place permanently as its own and make it a portion of its own country.

34.   As a general rule, the property belonging to churches, to hospitals, or other establishments of an exclusively charitable character, to establishments of education, or foundations for the promotion of knowledge, whether public schools, universities, academies of learning or observatories, museums of the fine arts, or of a scientific character—such property is not to be considered public property in the sense of paragraph 31; but it may be taxed or used when the public service may require it.

35. Classical works of art, libraries, scientific collections, or precious instruments, such as astronomical telescopes, as well as hospitals, must be secured against all avoidable injury, even when they are contained in fortified places whilst besieged or bombarded.

36. If such works of art, libraries, collections, or instruments belonging to a hostile nation or government, can be removed without injury, the ruler of the conquering state or nation may order them to be seized and removed for the benefit of the said nation. The ultimate ownership is to be settled by the ensuing treaty of peace.

In no case shall they be sold or given away, if captured by the armies of the United States, nor shall they ever be privately appropriated, or wantonly destroyed or injured.

37. The United States acknowledge and protect, in hostile countries occupied by them, religion and morality; strictly private property; the persons of the inhabitants, especially those of women; and the sacredness of domestic relations. Offenses to the contrary shall be rigorously punished.

This rule does not interfere with the right of the victorious invader to tax the people or their property, to levy forced loans, to billet soldiers, or to appropriate property, especially houses, lands, boats or ships, and the churches, for temporary and military uses.

38. Private property, unless forfeited by crimes or by offenses of the owner, can be seized only by way of military necessity, for the support or other benefit of the Army or of the United States.

If the owner has not fled, the commanding officer will cause receipts to be given, which may serve the spoliated owner to obtain indemnity.

39. The salaries of civil officers of the hostile government who remain in the invaded territory, and continue the work of their office, and can continue it according to the circumstances arising out of the war—such as judges, administrative or political officers, officers of city or communal governments—are paid from the public revenue of the invaded territory until the military government has reason wholly or partially to discontinue it. Salaries or incomes connected with purely honorary titles are always stopped.

40. There exists no law or body of authoritative rules of action between hostile armies, except that branch of the law of nature and nations which is called the law and usages of war on land.

41. All municipal law of the ground on which the armies stand, or of the countries to which they belong, is silent and of no effect between armies in the field.

42. Slavery, complicating and confounding the ideas of property (that is, of a thing), and of personality (that is, of humanity), exists according to municipal or local law only. The law of nature and nations has never acknowledged it. The digest of the Roman law enacts the early dictum of the pagan jurist, that "so far as the law of nature is concerned, all men are equal." Fugitives escaping from a country in which they were slaves, villains, or serfs, into another country, have, for centuries past, been held free and acknowledged free by judicial decisions of European countries, even though the municipal law of the country in which the slave had taken refuge acknowledged slavery within its own dominions.

43. Therefore, in a war between the United States and a belligerent which admits of slavery, if a person held in bondage by that belligerent be captured by or come as a fugitive under the protection of the military forces of the United States, such person is immediately entitled to the rights and privileges of a freeman. To return such person into slavery would amount to enslaving a free person, and neither the United States nor any officer under their authority can enslave any human being. Moreover, a person so made free by the law of war is under the shield of the law of nations, and the former owner or State can have, by the law of postliminy, no belligerent lien or claim of service.

44. All wanton violence committed against persons in the invaded country, all destruction of property not commanded by the authorized officer, all robbery, all pillage or sacking, even after taking a place by main force, all rape, wounding, maiming, or killing of such inhabitants, are prohibited under the penalty of death, or such other severe punishment as may seem adequate for the gravity of the offense.

A soldier, officer, or private, in the act of committing such violence, and disobeying a superior ordering him to abstain from it, may be lawfully killed on the spot by such superior.

45. All captures and booty belong, according to the modern law of war, primarily to the government of the captor.

Prize money, whether on sea or land, can now only be claimed under local law.

46. Neither officers nor soldiers are allowed to make use of their position or power in the hostile country for private gain, not even for commercial transactions otherwise legitimate. Offenses to the contrary

committed by commissioned officers will be punished with cashiering or such other punishment as the nature of the offense may require; if by soldiers, they shall be punished according to the nature of the offense.

47. Crimes punishable by all penal codes, such as arson, murder, maiming, assaults, highway robbery, theft, burglary, fraud, forgery, and rape, if committed by an American soldier in a hostile country against its inhabitants, are not only punishable as at home, but in all cases in which death is not inflicted the severer punishment shall be preferred.

SECTION III.—*Deserters—Prisoners of war—Hostages—Booty on the battle-field.*

48. Deserters from the American Army, having entered the service of the enemy, suffer death if they fall again into the hands of the United States, whether by capture or being delivered up to the American Army; and if a deserter from the enemy, having taken service in the Army of the United States, is captured by the enemy, and punished by them with death or otherwise, it is not a breach against the law and usages of war, requiring redress or retaliation.

49. A prisoner of war is a public enemy armed or attached to the hostile army for active aid, who has fallen into the hands of the captor, either fighting or wounded, on the field or in the hospital, by individual surrender or by capitulation.

All soldiers, of whatever species of arms; all men who belong to the rising *en masse* of the hostile country; all those who are attached to the Army for its efficiency and promote directly the object of the war, except such as are hereinafter provided for; all disabled men or officers on the field or elsewhere, if captured; all enemies who have thrown away their arms and ask for quarter, are prisoners of war, and as such exposed to the inconveniences as well as entitled to the privileges of a prisoner of war.

50. Moreover, citizens who accompany an army for whatever purpose, such as sutlers, editors, or reporters of journals, or contractors, if captured, may be made prisoners of war and be detained as such.

The monarch and members of the hostile reigning family, male or female, the chief, and chief officers of the hostile government, its diplomatic agents, and all persons who are of particular and singular use and benefit to the hostile army or its government, are, if captured on belligerent ground, and if unprovided with a safe-conduct granted by the captor's government, prisoners of war.

51.   If the people of that portion of an invaded country which is not yet occupied by the enemy, or of the whole country, at the approach of a hostile army, rise, under a duly authorized levy, *en masse* to resist the invader, they are now treated as public enemies, and, if captured, are prisoners of war.

52.   No belligerent has the right to declare that he will treat every captured man in arms of a levy *en masse* as a brigand or bandit.

If, however, the people of a country, or any portion of the same, already occupied by an army, rise against it, they are violators of the laws of war and are not entitled to their protection.

53.   The enemy's chaplains, officers of the medical staff, apothecaries, hospital nurses, and servants, if they fall into the hands of the American Army, are not prisoners of war, unless the commander has reasons to retain them. In this latter case, or if, at their own desire, they are allowed to remain with their captured companions, they are treated as prisoners of war, and may be exchanged if the commander sees fit.

54.   A hostage is a person accepted as a pledge for the fulfillment of an agreement concluded between belligerents during the war, or in consequence of a war. Hostages are rare in the present age.

55.   If a hostage is accepted, he is treated like a prisoner of war, according to rank and condition, as circumstances may admit.

56.   A prisoner of war is subject to no punishment for being a public enemy, nor is any revenge wreaked upon him by the intentional infliction of any suffering, or disgrace, by cruel imprisonment, want of food, by mutilation, death, or any other barbarity.

57.   So soon as a man is armed by a sovereign government and takes the soldier's oath of fidelity he is a belligerent; his killing, wounding, or other warlike acts are no individual crimes or offenses. No belligerent has a right to declare that enemies of a certain class, color, or condition, when properly organized as soldiers, will not be treated by him as public enemies.

58.   The law of nations knows of no distinction of color, and if an enemy of the United States should enslave and sell any captured persons of their Army, it would be a case for the severest retaliation, if not redressed upon complaint.

The United States cannot retaliate by enslavement; therefore death must be the retaliation for this crime against the law of nations.

59.   A prisoner of war remains answerable for his crimes

committed against the captor's army or people, committed before he was captured, and for which he has not been punished by his own authorities.

All prisoners of war are liable to the infliction of retaliatory measures.

60. It is against the usage of modern war to resolve, in hatred and revenge, to give no quarter. No body of troops has the right to declare that it will not give, and therefore will not expect, quarter; but a commander is permitted to direct his troops to give no quarter, in great straits, when his own salvation makes it impossible to cumber himself with prisoners.

61. Troops that give no quarter have no right to kill enemies already disabled on the ground, or prisoners captured by other troops.

62. All troops of the enemy known or discovered to give no quarter in general, or to any portion of the Army, receive none.

63. Troops who fight in the uniform of their enemies, without any plain, striking, and uniform mark of distinction of their own, can expect no quarter.

64. If American troops capture a train containing uniforms of the enemy, and the commander considers it advisable to distribute them for use among his men, some striking mark or sign must be adopted to distinguish the American soldier from the enemy.

65. The use of the enemy's national standard, flag, or other emblem of nationality, for the purpose of deceiving the enemy in battle, is an act of perfidy by which they lose all claim to the protection of the laws of war.

66. Quarter having been given to an enemy by American troops, under a misapprehension of his true character, he may, nevertheless, be ordered to suffer death if, within three days after the battle, it be discovered that he belongs to a corps which gives no quarter.

67. The law of nations allows every sovereign government to make war upon another sovereign State, and, therefore, admits of no rules or laws different from those of regular warfare, regarding the treatment of prisoners of war, although they may belong to the army of a government which the captor may consider as a wanton and unjust assailant.

68. Modern wars are not internecine wars, in which the killing of the enemy is the object. The destruction of the enemy in modern war, and, indeed, modern war itself, are means to obtain that object of the belligerent which lies beyond the war.

Unnecessary or revengeful destruction of life is not lawful.

69. Outposts, sentinels, or pickets are not to be fired upon, except to drive them in, or when a positive order, special or general, has been issued to that effect.

70. The use of poison in any manner, be it to poison wells, or food, or arms, is wholly excluded from modern warfare. He that uses it puts himself out of the pale of the law and usages of war.

71. Whoever intentionally inflicts additional wounds on an enemy already wholly disabled, or kills such an enemy, or who orders or encourages soldiers to do so, shall suffer death, if duly convicted, whether he belongs to the Army of the United States, or is an enemy captured after having committed his misdeed.

72. Money and other valuables on the person of a prisoner, such as watches or jewelry, as well as extra clothing, are regarded by the American Army as the private property of the prisoner, and the appropriation of such valuables or money is considered dishonorable, and is prohibited.

Nevertheless, if large sums are found upon the persons of prisoners, or in their possession, they shall be taken from them, and the surplus, after providing for their own support, appropriated for the use of the Army, under the direction of the commander, unless otherwise ordered by the Government. Nor can prisoners claim, as private property, large sums found and captured in their train, although they have been placed in the private luggage of the prisoners.

73. All officers, when captured, must surrender their side-arms to the captor. They may be restored to the prisoner in marked cases, by the commander, to signalize admiration of his distinguished bravery, or approbation of his humane treatment of prisoners before his capture. The captured officer to whom they may be restored cannot wear them during captivity.

74. A prisoner of war, being a public enemy, is the prisoner of the Government and not of the captor. No ransom can be paid by a prisoner of war to his individual captor, or to any officer in command. The Government alone releases captives, according to rules prescribed by itself.

75. Prisoners of war are subject to confinement or imprisonment such as may be deemed necessary on account of safety, but they are to be subjected to no other intentional suffering or indignity. The confinement and mode of treating a prisoner may be varied during his captivity according to the demands of safety.

76. Prisoners of war shall be fed upon plain and wholesome food, whenever practicable, and treated with humanity.

They may be required to work for the benefit of the captor's government, according to their rank and condition.

77. A prisoner of war who escapes may be shot, or otherwise killed, in his flight; but neither death nor any other punishment shall be inflicted upon him simply for his attempt to escape, which the law of war does not consider a crime. Stricter means of security shall be used after an unsuccessful attempt at escape.

If, however, a conspiracy is discovered, the purpose of which is a united or general escape, the conspirators may be rigorously punished, even with death; and capital punishment may also be inflicted upon prisoners of war discovered to have plotted rebellion against the authorities of the captors, whether in union with fellow-prisoners or other persons.

78. If prisoners of war, having given no pledge nor made any promise on their honor, forcibly or otherwise escape, and are captured again in battle, after having rejoined their own army, they shall not be punished for their escape, but shall be treated as simple prisoners of war, although they will be subjected to stricter confinement.

79. Every captured wounded enemy shall be medically treated, according to the ability of the medical staff.

80. Honorable men, when captured, will abstain from giving to the enemy information concerning their own army, and the modern law of war permits no longer the use of any violence against prisoners in order to extort the desired information, or to punish them for having given false information.

SECTION IV.—*Partisans—Armed enemies not belonging to the hostile army—Scouts—Armed prowlers—War-rebels.*

81. Partisans are soldiers armed and wearing the uniform of their army, but belonging to a corps which acts detached from the main body for the purpose of making inroads into the territory occupied by the enemy. If captured they are entitled to all the privileges of the prisoner of war.

82. Men, or squads of men, who commit hostilities, whether by fighting, or inroads for destruction or plunder, or by raids of any kind, without commission, without being part and portion of the organized hostile army, and without sharing continuously in the war, but who do so with intermitting returns to their homes and avocations, or with the occasional assumption of the semblance of peaceful pursuits, divesting themselves of the character or appearance of soldiers—such men, or squads of men, are not public enemies, and therefore, if captured, are

not entitled to the privileges of prisoners of war, but shall be treated summarily as highway robbers or pirates.

83. Scouts or single soldiers, if disguised in the dress of the country, or in the uniform of the army hostile to their own, employed in obtaining information, if found within or lurking about the lines of the captor, are treated as spies, and suffer death.

84. Armed prowlers, by whatever names they may be called, or persons of the enemy's territory, who steal within the lines of the hostile army for the purpose of robbing, killing, or of destroying bridges, roads, or canals, or of robbing or destroying the mail, or of cutting the telegraph wires, are not entitled to the privileges of the prisoner of war.

85. War-rebels are persons within an occupied territory who rise in arms against the occupying or conquering army, or against the authorities established by the same. If captured, they may suffer death, whether they rise singly, in small or large bands, and whether called upon to do so by their own, but expelled, government or not. They are not prisoners of war; nor are they if discovered and secured before their conspiracy has matured to an actual rising or to armed violence.

SECTION V.—*Safe-conduct—Spies—War-traitors—Captured messengers—Abuse of the flag of truce.*

86. All intercourse between the territories occupied by belligerent armies, whether by traffic, by letter, by travel, or in any other way, ceases. This is the general rule, to be observed without special proclamation.

Exceptions to this rule, whether by safe-conduct or permission to trade on a small or large scale, or by exchanging mails, or by travel from one territory into the other, can take place only according to agreement approved by the Government or by the highest military authority.

Contraventions of this rule are highly punishable.

87. Ambassadors, and all other diplomatic agents of neutral powers accredited to the enemy may receive safe-conducts through the territories occupied by the belligerents, unless there are military reasons to the contrary, and unless they may reach the place of their destination conveniently by another route. It implies no international affront if the safe-conduct is declined. Such passes are usually given by the supreme authority of the state and not by subordinate officers.

88. A spy is a person who secretly, in disguise or under false

pretense, seeks information with the intention of communicating it to the enemy.

The spy is punishable with death by hanging by the neck, whether or not he succeed in obtaining the information or in conveying it to the enemy.

89. If a citizen of the United States obtains information in a legitimate manner and betrays it to the enemy, be he a military or civil officer, or a private citizen, he shall suffer death.

90. A traitor under the law of war, or a war-traitor, is a person in a place or district under martial law who, unauthorized by the military commander, gives information of any kind to the enemy, or holds intercourse with him.

91. The war-traitor is always severely punished. If his offense consists in betraying to the enemy anything concerning the condition, safety, operations, or plans of the troops holding or occupying the place or district, his punishment is death.

92. If the citizen or subject of a country or place invaded or conquered gives information to his own government, from which he is separated by the hostile army, or to the army of his government, he is a war-traitor, and death is the penalty of his offense.

93. All armies in the field stand in need of guides, and impress them if they cannot obtain them otherwise.

94. No person having been forced by the enemy to serve as guide is punishable for having done so.

95. If a citizen of a hostile and invaded district voluntarily serves as a guide to the enemy, or offers to do so, he is deemed a war-traitor and shall suffer death.

96. A citizen serving voluntarily as a guide against his own country commits treason, and will be dealt with according to the law of his country.

97. Guides, when it is clearly proved that they have misled intentionally, may be put to death.

98. All unauthorized or secret communication with the enemy is considered treasonable by the law of war.

Foreign residents in an invaded or occupied territory or foreign visitors in the same can claim no immunity from this law. They may communicate with foreign parts or with the inhabitants of the hostile

country, so far as the military authority permits, but no further. Instant expulsion from the occupied territory would be the very least punishment for the infraction of this rule.

99. A messenger carrying written dispatches or verbal messages from one portion of the army or from a besieged place to another portion of the same army or its government, if armed, and in the uniform of his army, and if captured while doing so in the territory occupied by the enemy, is treated by the captor as a prisoner of war. If not in uniform nor a soldier, the circumstances connected with his capture must determine the disposition that shall be made of him.

100. A messenger or agent who attempts to steal through the territory occupied by the enemy to further in any manner the interests of the enemy, if captured, is not entitled to the privileges of the prisoner of war, and may be dealt with according to the circumstances of the case.

101. While deception in war is admitted as a just and necessary means of hostility, and is consistent with honorable warfare, the common law of war allows even capital punishment for clandestine or treacherous attempts to injure an enemy, because they are so dangerous, and it is so difficult to guard against them.

102. The law of war, like the criminal law regarding other offenses, makes no difference on account of the difference of sexes, concerning the spy, the war-traitor, or the war-rebel.

103. Spies, war-traitors, and war-rebels are not exchanged according to the common law of war. The exchange of such persons would require a special cartel, authorized by the Government, or, at a great distance from it, by the chief commander of the army in the field.

104. A successful spy or war-traitor, safely returned to his own army, and afterward captured as an enemy, is not subject to punishment for his acts as a spy or war-traitor, but he may be held in closer custody as a person individually dangerous.

SECTION VI.—*Exchange of prisoners—Flags of truce—Flags of protection.*

105. Exchanges of prisoners take place—number for number—rank for rank—wounded for wounded—with added condition for added condition—such, for instance, as not to serve for a certain period.

106. In exchanging prisoners of war, such numbers of persons of inferior rank may be substituted as an equivalent for one of superior rank as may be agreed upon by cartel, which requires the sanction of the Government, or of the commander of the army in the field.

107. A prisoner of war is in honor bound truly to state to the captor his rank; and he is not to assume a lower rank than belongs to him, in order to cause a more advantageous exchange, nor a higher rank, for the purpose of obtaining better treatment.

Offenses to the contrary have been justly punished by the commanders of released prisoners, and may be good cause for refusing to release such prisoners.

108. The surplus number of prisoners of war remaining after an exchange has taken place is sometimes released either for the payment of a stipulated sum of money, or, in urgent cases, of provision, clothing, or other necessaries.

Such arrangement, however, requires the sanction of the highest authority.

109. The exchange of prisoners of war is an act of convenience to both belligerents. If no general cartel has been concluded, it cannot be demanded by either of them. No belligerent is obliged to exchange prisoners of war.

A cartel is voidable as soon as either party has violated it.

110. No exchange of prisoners shall be made except after complete capture, and after an accurate account of them, and a list of the captured officers, has been taken.

111. The bearer of a flag of truce cannot insist upon being admitted. He must always be admitted with great caution. Unnecessary frequency is carefully to be avoided.

112. If the bearer of a flag of truce offer himself during an engagement, he can be admitted as a very rare exception only. It is no breach of good faith to retain such flag of truce, if admitted during the engagement. Firing is not required to cease on the appearance of a flag of truce in battle.

113. If the bearer of a flag of truce, presenting himself during an engagement, is killed or wounded, it furnishes no ground of complaint whatever.

114. If it be discovered, and fairly proved, that a flag of truce has been abused for surreptitiously obtaining military knowledge, the bearer of the flag thus abusing his sacred character is deemed a spy.

So sacred is the character of a flag of truce, and so necessary is its sacredness, that while its abuse is an especially heinous offense, great caution is requisite, on the other hand, in convicting the bearer of a flag of truce as a spy.

115. It is customary to designate by certain flags (usually yellow) the hospitals in places which are shelled, so that the besieging enemy may avoid firing on them. The same has been done in battles when hospitals are situated within the field of the engagement.

116. Honorable belligerents often request that the hospitals within the territory of the enemy may be designated, so that they may be spared.

An honorable belligerent allows himself to be guided by flags or signals of protection as much as the contingencies and the necessities of the fight will permit.

117. It is justly considered an act of bad faith, of infamy or fiendishness, to deceive the enemy by flags of protection. Such act of bad faith may be good cause for refusing to respect such flags.

118. The besieging belligerent has sometimes requested the besieged to designate the buildings containing collections of works of art, scientific museums, astronomical observatories, or precious libraries, so that their destruction may be avoided as much as possible.

SECTION VII.—*The parole.*

119. Prisoners of war may be released from captivity by exchange, and, under certain circumstances, also by parole.

120. The term parole designates the pledge of individual good faith and honor to do, or to omit doing, certain acts after he who gives his parole shall have been dismissed, wholly or partially, from the power of the captor.

121. The pledge of the parole is always an individual, but not a private act.

122. The parole applies chiefly to prisoners of war whom the captor allows to return to their country, or to live in greater freedom within the captor's country or territory, on conditions stated in the parole.

123. Release of prisoners of war by exchange is the general rule; release by parole is the exception.

124. Breaking the parole is punished with death when the person breaking the parole is captured again.

Accurate lists, therefore, of the paroled persons must be kept by the belligerents.

125. When paroles are given and received there must be an exchange of two written documents, in which the name and rank of the paroled individuals are accurately and truthfully stated.

126. Commissioned officers only are allowed to give their parole, and they can give it only with the permission of their superior, as long as a superior in rank is within reach.

127. No non-commissioned officer or private can give his parole except through an officer. Individual paroles not given through an officer are not only void, but subject the individuals giving them to the punishment of death as deserters. The only admissible exception is where individuals, properly separated from their commands, have suffered long confinement without the possibility of being paroled through an officer.

128. No paroling on the battle-field; no paroling of entire bodies of troops after a battle; and no dismissal of large numbers of prisoners, with a general declaration that they are paroled, is permitted, or of any value.

129. In capitulations for the surrender of strong places or fortified camps the commanding officer, in cases of urgent necessity, may agree that the troops under his command shall not fight again during the war unless exchanged.

130. The usual pledge given in the parole is not to serve during the existing war unless exchanged.

This pledge refers only to the active service in the field against the paroling belligerent or his allies actively engaged in the same war. These cases of breaking the parole are patent acts, and can be visited with the punishment of death; but the pledge does not refer to internal service, such as recruiting or drilling the recruits, fortifying places not besieged, quelling civil commotions, fighting against belligerents unconnected with the paroling belligerents, or to civil or diplomatic service for which the paroled officer may be employed.

131. If the government does not approve of the parole, the paroled officer must return into captivity, and should the enemy refuse to receive him he is free of his parole.

132. A belligerent government may declare, by a general order, whether it will allow paroling and on what conditions it will allow it. Such order is communicated to the enemy.

133. No prisoner of war can be forced by the hostile government to parole himself, and no government is obliged to parole prisoners of war or to parole all captured officers, if it paroles any. As the pledging of the parole is an individual act, so is paroling, on the other hand, an act of choice on the part of the belligerent.

134. The commander of an occupying army may require of the civil officers of the enemy, and of its citizens, any pledge he may consider

necessary for the safety or security of his army, and upon their failure to give it he may arrest, confine, or detain them.

SECTION VIII.—*Armistice—Capitulation.*

135. An armistice is the cessation of active hostilities for a period agreed between belligerents. It must be agreed upon in writing and duly ratified by the highest authorities of the contending parties.

136. If an armistice be declared without conditions it extends no further than to require a total cessation of hostilities along the front of both belligerents.

If conditions be agreed upon, they should be clearly expressed, and must be rigidly adhered to by both parties. If either party violates any express condition, the armistice may be declared null and void by the other.

137. An armistice may be general, and valid for all points and lines of the belligerents; or special—that is, referring to certain troops or certain localities only. An armistice may be concluded for a definite time; or for an indefinite time, during which either belligerent may resume hostilities on giving the notice agreed upon to the other.

138. The motives which induce the one or the other belligerent to conclude an armistice, whether it be expected to be preliminary to a treaty of peace, or to prepare during the armistice for a more vigorous prosecution of the war, does in no way affect the character of the armistice itself.

139. An armistice is binding upon the belligerents from the day of the agreed commencement; but the officers of the armies are responsible from the day only when they receive official information of its existence.

140. Commanding officers have the right to conclude armistices binding on the district over which their command extends, but such armistice is subject to the ratification of the superior authority, and ceases so soon as it is made known to the enemy that the armistice is not ratified, even if a certain time for the elapsing between giving notice of cessation and the resumption of hostilities should have been stipulated for.

141. It is incumbent upon the contracting parties of an armistice to stipulate what intercourse of persons or traffic between the inhabitants of the territories occupied by the hostile armies shall be allowed, if any.

If nothing is stipulated the intercourse remains suspended, as during actual hostilities.

142. An armistice is not a partial or a temporary peace; it is only

the suspension of military operations to the extent agreed upon by the parties.

143. When an armistice is concluded between a fortified place and the army besieging it, it is agreed by all the authorities on this subject that the besieger must cease all extension, perfection, or advance of his attacking works as much so as from attacks by main force.

But as there is a difference of opinion among martial jurists whether the besieged have a right to repair breaches or to erect new works of defense within the place during an armistice, this point should be determined by express agreement between the parties.

144. So soon as a capitulation is signed the capitulator has no right to demolish, destroy, or injure the works, arms, stores, or ammunition in his possession, during the time which elapses between the signing and the execution of the capitulation, unless otherwise stipulated in the same.

145. When an armistice is clearly broken by one of the parties the other party is released from all obligation to observe it.

146. Prisoners taken in the act of breaking an armistice must be treated as prisoners of war, the officer alone being responsible who gives the order for such a violation of an armistice. The highest authority of the belligerent aggrieved may demand redress for the infraction of an armistice.

147. Belligerents sometimes conclude an armistice while their plenipotentiaries are met to discuss the conditions of a treaty of peace; but plenipotentiaries may meet without a preliminary armistice; in the latter case the war is carried on without any abatement.

SECTION IX.—*Assassination.*

148. The law of war does not allow proclaiming either an individual belonging to the hostile army, or a citizen, or a subject of the hostile government an outlaw, who may be slain without trial by any captor, any more than the modern law of peace allows such international outlawry; on the contrary, it abhors such outrage. The sternest retaliation should follow the murder committed in consequence of such proclamation, made by whatever authority. Civilized nations look with horror upon offers of rewards for the assassination of enemies as relapses into barbarism.

SECTION X.—*Insurrection—Civil war—Rebellion.*

149. Insurrection is the rising of people in arms against their government, or portion of it, or against one or more of its laws, or against an

officer or officers of the government. It may be confined to mere armed resistance, or it may have greater ends in view.

150. Civil war is war between two or more portions of a country or state, each contending for the mastery of the whole, and each claiming to be the legitimate government. The term is also sometimes applied to war of rebellion, when the rebellious provinces or portions of the state are contiguous to those containing the seat of government.

151. The term rebellion is applied to an insurrection of large extent, and is usually a war between the legitimate government of a country and portions of provinces of the same who seek to throw off their allegiance to it and set up a government of their own.

152. When humanity induces the adoption of the rules of regular war toward rebels, whether the adoption is partial or entire, it does in no way whatever imply a partial or complete acknowledgment of their government, if they have set up one, or of them, as an independent or sovereign power. Neutrals have no right to make the adoption of the rules of war by the assailed government toward rebels the ground of their own acknowledgment of the revolted people as an independent power.

153. Treating captured rebels as prisoners of war, exchanging them, concluding of cartels, capitulations, or other warlike agreements with them; addressing officers of a rebel army by the rank they may have in the same; accepting flags of truce; or, on the other hand, proclaiming martial law in their territory, or levying war taxes or forced loans, or doing any other act sanctioned or demanded by the law and usages of public war between sovereign belligerents, neither proves nor establishes an acknowledgment of the rebellious people, or of the government which they may have erected, as a public or sovereign power. Nor does the adoption of the rules of war toward rebels imply an engagement with them extending beyond the limits of these rules. It is victory in the field that ends the strife and settles the future relations between the contending parties.

154. Treating in the field the rebellious enemy according to the law and usages of war has never prevented the legitimate government from trying the leaders of the rebellion or chief rebels for high treason, and from treating them accordingly, unless they are included in a general amnesty.

155. All enemies in regular war are divided into two general classes—that is to say, into combatants and non-combatants, or unarmed citizens of the hostile government.

The military commander of the legitimate government, in a war of rebellion, distinguishes between the loyal citizen in the revolted

portion of the country and the disloyal citizen. The disloyal citizens may further be classified into those citizens known to sympathize with the rebellion without positively aiding it, and those who, without taking up arms, give positive aid and comfort to the rebellious enemy without being bodily forced thereto.

156. Common justice and plain expediency require that the military commander protect the manifestly loyal citizens in revolted territories against the hardships of the war as much as the common misfortune of all war admits.

The commander will throw the burden of the war, as much as lies within his power, on the disloyal citizens, of the revolted portion or province, subjecting them to a stricter police than the non-combatant enemies have to suffer in regular war; and if he deems it appropriate, or if his government demands of him that every citizen shall, by an oath of allegiance, or by some other manifest act, declare his fidelity to the legitimate government, he may expel, transfer, imprison, or fine the revolted citizens who refuse to pledge themselves anew as citizens obedient to the law and loyal to the government.

Whether it is expedient to do so, and whether reliance can be placed upon such oaths, the commander or his government have the right to decide.

157. Armed or unarmed resistance by citizens of the United States against the lawful movements of their troops is levying war against the United States, and is therefore treason.

About the Author

Robert D. Ramsey III retired from the US Army in 1993 after 24 years of service as an Infantry officer that included tours in Vietnam, Korea, and the Sinai. He earned an M.A. in history from Rice University. Mr. Ramsey taught military history for 3 years at the United States Military Academy and 6 years at the US Army Command and General Staff College. Mr. Ramsey is the author of Global War on Terrorism Occasional Paper 18, *Advising Indigenous Forces: American Advisors in Korea, Vietnam, and El Salvador;* Occasional Paper 19, *Advice for Advisors: Suggestions and Observations from Lawrence to the Present;* and Occasional Paper 24, *Savage Wars of Peace: Case Studies of Pacification in the Philippines, 1900–1902.*